OUR FRUITS OF CHRISTIANITY

FOUNDATIONS

A 31-DAY DEVOTIONAL

POWER HOUSE

Our Fruits of Christianity

FOUNDATIONS

A 31-DAY DEVOTIONAL

TAMRA INGRAM-CURRY

Cover and Interior Design by Dr. Michelle Everett for POWER HOUSE

Published by: Power House

An imprint of Power House Studios LLC.

thepowerhousestudio.com

PO Box 101678

Cape Coral FL 33910

Home of *The Power House Blueprint*™ Concierge Publishing System

CONTENTS

INTRODUCTION

Welcome to *Foundations,* the first book in the *Our Fruits of Christianity* devotional series. Within *Foundations,* we identify the most basic *fruits* we can experience and enjoy in our lives as Christians. The goal of this book (and the others in the series) is not to place boundaries on a Christian's life; instead, it is to celebrate some of the natural and spiritual gifts that come as a result of orderliness and perseverance in a life lived according to the Bible. Please note that this is not a series on "the fruit of the Spirit," specifically as listed in Galatians 5:22–23. However, the fruit described and given through the direction of the Holy Spirit in the Galatians passage influences and develops the many fruits of our Christianity. Allow me to explain.

This devotion does not tell you *how to live* but gives examples of fruit (visual or palatable and physical results) that many Christians experience, not fruit you *should be* experiencing.

In John 15:5, Jesus said, "I am the vine, you are the branches. He who abides in Me, and I in him, bears much fruit; for without Me you can do nothing." As branches, we all grow differently off the vine. Our job isn't to dictate what we produce but rather to cling tightly to The Vine and allow God to minister to each of us individually according to the call He has placed on our lives. Many times, this growth births fruit for us to enjoy and even share with the rest of the Body of Christ. As a physical human body has many parts, the Body of Christ has many parts. These parts are people who give expression to the various gifts, talents, and calls given directly from God the Father, the Vine-dresser (John 15:1). The fruit of our Christianity is for recognition, for use, and spiritual food.

Each daily topic is scripture-rich. Some topics will reflect journeys you have already experienced, and others may be things that God is presenting to you for development. None of the fruits discussed should be viewed as things a believer *must produce*; instead, they are attributes that *God directs* in His perfect order and timing through the vine-branch connection.

Although each book in the series may be used as a stand-alone study, a companion study journal is available for each book. It includes challenge questions to extend each day's devotional if desired. You may discover that you enjoy using the journal in a variety of additional ways. Here are some ideas:

- Use both the devotional reading and the companion journal with the challenge questions on the same day for a more extended study period.

- Spread out the devotional studies into two days per reading. On the first day, read the devotional text and allow it to sink in for the first twenty-four hours; then, on the next day, go to the corresponding journal entry to further study and complete the challenge questions before moving forward.

- Share the devotional as a small group. Group members can read the devotional text each day, and journal entries and challenge questions can be used as a part of the group discussion.

I thank you for your purchase, and I pray this prayer for each person who endeavors to study God's Word through this devotional series:

> For this reason we also, since the day we heard it, do not cease to pray for you, and to ask that you may be filled with the knowledge of His will in all wisdom and spiritual understanding; that you may walk worthy of the Lord, fully pleasing Him, being fruitful in every good work and increasing in the knowledge of God; strengthened with all might, according to His glorious power, for all patience and longsuffering with joy; giving thanks to the Father who has qualified us to be partakers of the inheritance of the saints in the light. He has delivered us from the power of darkness and conveyed us into the kingdom of the Son of His love, in whom we have redemption through His blood, the forgiveness of sins. (Colossians 1:9–14)

I pray the reading of this devotional blesses you and causes you to grow in Christ through its simple presentation.

Warmest regards,

Tamra Ingram-Curry

DAY 1

— OUR FRUIT OF STANDING —

STANDING DAILY

As we explore *Our Fruit of Standing*, let us first establish how the dictionary defines the word *stand*. Used as a verb, to stand is to be submitted to, to withstand, put up with, tolerate, endure, act as or in place of another.[1] Synonyms for the word *stand* are tolerate, suffer, stay, remain, sustain, rest. Antonyms for the word *stand* are run, yield, advance.[2]

For our study today, to stand is to be upright on one's feet, rise to one's feet; to be upright, be in a certain place, rank, or scale. To stand is to take or keep a certain position; take away to thinking or acting; be in a *special* condition; To stand is to *be unchanged, hold good, remain the same; resist destruction or decay*; to stand is to collect and remain; to *take or remain in a certain course or direction*; to stop moving, halt, or to stop.[3]

In Scripture, we can find the word *stand* used in these verses (among others):

> And Moses said unto the people, fear ye not, *stand still* and see the salvation of the Lord, which he will show to you today: for the Egyptians whom ye have seen today, ye shall see them again no more forever. (Exodus 14:13 KJ21; emphasis added)

> Happy are thy men, happy are these, thy servants, which *stand continually* before thee, and that hear thy wisdom. (1 Kings 10:8 KJ21; emphasis added)

> Who shall ascend into the hill of the Lord? Or who shall *stand in his holy place*? (Psalm 24:3 KJ21; emphasis added)

> Take hold of shield and buckler, and *stand up* for mine help. (Psalm 35:2 KJ21; emphasis added)

> "*Stand ye in the ways*, and see, and ask for the old paths, where is the good way, and walk therein, and ye shall find rest for your souls." But they said, "We will not walk there in." (Jeremiah 6:16 KJ21; emphasis added)

Watch ye, *stand fast in the faith*, quit you like
men, be strong. (1 Corinthians 16:13 KJ21;
emphasis added)

Wherefore take unto you the whole armor of
God, that *ye may be able to withstand* in the evil
day, *and having done all, to stand.* (Ephesians
6:13 KJ21; emphasis added)

In order to stand, we must first recognize our need to do so!
We must learn to identify the enemy and his schemes and the
games he tries to pull. As we identify his threats, then we must
actively stand against the enemy with The Word of God so that
the enemy will flee. Years ago (2007), I wrote down a powerful
statement spoken by a pastor in Harrison, Arkansas, and I have
kept the quote all these years:

Satan fears detection most of all. And he hates
confrontation with a believer. Satan knows the
integrity of God. Satan fears our discovery of
God's Word and our believing His word. ~ Rev.
Arlis Thrasher

Standing is not always an easy way to live. It doesn't have
to be a minute-by-minute conscious activity, but it must be a
daily action. It will get easier to recognize the attacks from the
real enemy, satan, but the attacks will not stop while we are on
the earth (which is temporarily his domain of rule).

One tool we can employ against the enemy is to make memory our servant against mental attacks. We can command the mind to recall, to bring the Word to our remembrance so that we can use it as a shield. It is especially true of how God has already given you and me the victory over satan. When we remember that we have victory in Christ, it is easier to stand and to praise God *as we stand*.

Three main things will help you stand and allow your spiritual legs to gain strength to do so:

- Pray daily.

- Fast.

- Know and memorize Scripture through daily reading and meditating in the Bible, then quote it out loud.

PRAYER

Father, help us to know what a valuable fruit standing can be to the Christian. May we gain a new understanding of how to stand and how to comprehend the goodness of the Lord! Even as we walk in the land of the wicked, help us to do so without hesitation and fear because we are in Christ and the fullness of Him. We ask you to give us, Lord, this understanding of how to stand. Thank you for this gift. Amen.

DAY 2

— OUR FRUIT OF STANDING —

STANDING FAST

Standing is visible or evidenced when we maintain our position in God, remain in faith, and proclaim our Christian beliefs. Standing is the spiritual warfare Christians are to live out. Standing is remaining unmoved by things around us, remaining steadfast, believing the Word of God, and resisting Satan's destruction and decay in our lives.

In the verses below (and others), we can see that the Bible instructs us to stand:

> Only let your manner of living be as becometh the Gospel of Christ, that whether I come and see you or else am absent, I may hear of your affairs that ye *stand fast* in one spirit, with one

mind, striving together of the faith of the Gospel. (Philippians 1:27 KJV21; emphasis added)

Therefore, my brethren dearly beloved and longed for, my joy and crown, so *stand fast* in the Lord, my dearly beloved. (Philippians 4:1 KJV; emphasis added)

For now we live, if ye *stand fast* in the Lord. (1 Thessalonians 3:8 KJV; emphasis added)

Therefore submit to God. *Resist the devil, and he will flee from you.* (James 4:7; emphasis added)

Resist, by definition, means to fight, withstand the action or effect of, or refrain from doing or having (something tempting or unwise).[4] Oxford Languages defines *resist* in the noun form as a resistant substance applied as a coating to protect a surface during some process [as in printing or ceramics].[5]

Looking at that definition in the spiritual sense, we could say that the Word of God represents that resistant substance, our layer of protection from the snares of the enemy. We only have one enemy, satan. The Bible tells us that we don't wrestle with flesh and blood (people and natural things) but with principalities and powers in the heavens (the atmosphere). That references the supernatural and spiritual realm. We must resist (in the action verb form) him, and he must flee!

PRAYER

Father, help us monitor our daily conversations so that they reflect the power you implanted in us. Help us to use Your Word to stand firm, trust in You, and ever-increasing in our understanding of Your Word. Help us to memorize Your Word and gain knowledge of our position in faith and our beliefs, not wavering or being double-minded. May we resist the suggestions and plans of the enemy in our lives through a clear understanding of You—who You are to us—keeping us steadfast and unchangeable in You. Thank you for this fruit of standing firm in Christ. Amen.

DAY 3
— OUR FRUIT OF STANDING —
STAND BY KNOWING THE WORD

Did you know that involving more of our senses like seeing, hearing, speaking, touching the page, etc. as we study helps us to retain what we study? For example, the Bible tells us in Romans 10:17, "So then Faith comes by hearing, and hearing by the Word of God." The Word of God also says in Romans 12:3, "God has dealt to each one a measure of Faith." That means our faith comes from the Bible itself. It comes from those speaking, preaching, and teaching the Bible. It also comes by hearing the Word of God, so reading the scriptures regularly out loud, where our ears can hear, builds our faith.

The best way to stand against the devil is to meditate daily on the Word of God. Memorizing the Word of God is another great way to have it ready to use anytime you are under attack. We gain strength by using our weapon, the Sword which is the

Word of God. If you need faith to walk strong in a particular area or challenge, seek out verses about that topic or need, agree with the Word, and learn to put it to use in your daily life just like Jesus did.

Here are a few supporting Scriptures about standing:

> And Moses said unto them, *stand still,* and I will hear what the Lord will command concerning you. (Numbers 9:8 KJV; emphasis added)

> *Stand in awe,* and sin not: commune with your own heart upon your bed, and be still. Selah. (Psalm 4:4 KJV; emphasis added)

> Not for that we have dominion over your faith, but are helpers of your joy: for *by faith ye stand.* (2 Corinthians 1:24 KJV; emphasis added)

We also see in the New Testament that Jesus stood against the adversary, whom the Bible also calls our enemy, satan, the devourer. We can learn so much about *standing* from His pattern of standing against satan in the passages from Matthew 4:1–11 (emphasis added):

> Then Jesus was led up by the Spirit into the wilderness to be tempted by the devil. And when He had fasted forty days and forty nights, afterward He was hungry. Now when the tempt-

16

er came to Him, he said, "If You are the Son of God, command that these stones become bread." But He answered and said, "*It is written*, 'Man shall not live by bread alone, but by every word that proceeds from the mouth of God.' "

Then the devil took Him up into the holy city, set Him on the pinnacle of the temple, and said to Him, "If You are the Son of God, throw Yourself down. For it is written: 'He shall give His angels charge over you,' and, 'In their hands they shall bear you up, Lest you dash your foot against a stone.' " Jesus said to him, "*It is written again*, 'You shall not tempt the Lord your God.' "

Again, the devil took Him up on an exceedingly high mountain, and showed Him all the kingdoms of the world and their glory. And he said to Him, "All these things I will give You if You will fall down and worship me."

Then Jesus said to him, "Away with you, Satan! *For it is written*, 'You shall worship the Lord your God, and Him only you shall serve.' " Then the devil left Him, and behold, angels came and ministered to Him.

You see, many people don't stand against the enemy because they either don't realize there is an enemy or they have no idea they could stand against him. But once you know about something (get understanding), you tend to have faith for that thing. That is how it is in learning to *stand*.

As you learn the Word about *standing in faith*, you actually have more faith to do so! You might think of it like this: when I hadn't yet developed my driving skills, I was apprehensive about getting behind the steering wheel. However, after I learned how to drive, I believed I could drive anywhere.

Similarly, in the same way that we realize that one should never ride with a person who doesn't know how to drive and operate a vehicle; you should also never sit under some pastor who doesn't teach the Word in its fullness. Not knowing the Bible in its fullness makes for a weak soldier of God, or in the case of our car analogy, is a wreck waiting to happen. You cannot effectively stand without the Word of God.

Jesus Christ is our example—this is our fruit of being a Christian—whatever we see Jesus doing in Scripture, that is our pattern. We are in a battle, but in reality, we are fighting to believe that *it's already won*. The truth is that Jesus won it on the Cross. He declared as He said, "It is finished."

> After this, Jesus, *knowing that all things were now accomplished, that the Scripture might be fulfilled,* said, "I thirst!" Now a vessel full of sour wine was sitting there; and they filled a sponge with sour wine, put it on hyssop, and put it to

His mouth. So when Jesus had received the sour wine, He said, "*It is finished!*" And bowing His head, He gave up His spirit. (John 19:28–30; emphasis added)

Remember, the war was finished; sin was finished; the separation between God and His creation of man was finished; sickness was finished; poverty was finished. And satan was finished at that moment. **Jesus took care of it all on the Cross.** There is not one thing we must do *except stand in faith!* That is our fight of faith. To stand is to have faith in what Jesus finished!

PRAYER

Father, I ask that You teach us through the Holy Scriptures to stand firm in your Word. Reveal the hidden treasures of your Word that help us to live in agreement with your Word and make better choices in life and circumstances. Help us to recognize the enemy through the understanding and knowledge of the scriptures; help us to know that the enemy is not a creative being but a repeater of accusations and sin. Show us how to gain strength against his plans for us through your Holy Scriptures and how to hide your Word in our hearts and minds as a storehouse of resources for daily use. In the name of Jesus, I ask for this. Amen.

DAY 4

— OUR FRUIT OF STANDING —

STANDING IN OUR ARMOR

Standing implies a defensive stance against something attacking what is rightfully ours. We can find each spiritual weapon that God has provided to *the saints* (the people of God) in Ephesians 6:10–18 (emphasis added):

> Finally, my brethren, be strong in the Lord and in the power of His might. **Put on the whole armor of God, that *you may be able to stand against the wiles of the devil.*** For we do not wrestle against flesh and blood, but against principalities, against powers, against the rulers of the darkness of this age, against spiritual hosts of wickedness in the heavenly places. Therefore take up the whole armor of God,

that you may be able to withstand in the evil day, and having done all, to stand.

Stand therefore, having girded your waist with truth, having put on the breastplate of righteousness, and having shod your feet with the preparation of the gospel of peace; above all, taking the shield of faith with which you will be able to quench all the fiery darts of the wicked one. And take the helmet of salvation, and the sword of the Spirit, which is the word of God; praying always with all prayer and supplication in the Spirit, being watchful to this end with all perseverance and supplication for all *the saints*—

God gave each believer this *whole armor*, these powerful equippings, as a gift. They belong to all the saints—every believer in Christ. We can use them as needed—each spiritual weapon is available every minute of every day to those who are His own.

It is valuable to take the time to study the historical armor and uniform of a Roman soldier. I recommend it as a beneficial extra study after completing this devotional. To touch on it briefly, as we consider the natural pieces of armor, we can take note of the protective coverings and the weapons Roman soldiers used at that time. As we look at the armor, we can think about how it applies to the spiritual realm.

For example, we can better understand our spiritual armor by considering the function and effect of each piece of natural armor. Which piece affects which part of the body and the body as a whole? What is the function and the protection provided by each piece? The Bible frequently uses the image of what we can see to teach us about the principles of things we cannot yet see. It is astounding what spiritual insight we can gain from these details!

The reason we don't get issued a physical helmet, belt, boots, etc., when we become a Christian is because *our fight is spiritual.* When the Bible tells us the fight is not against flesh and blood, this means we are not in this fight against other humans! It is vital to keep this in mind when we come up against the adversary operating *through a human.* It's not the physical person we are to fight against. Many who come against us don't even realize they have been deceived and are being used by the enemy. Always separate the sin from the person. We are to have great compassion for the person; still, we should expose deception and sin properly, spiritually, discreetly, and *in love.* Remember, love is our commandment and law today. Love people, oppose (stand fiercely against) the enemy. As we learn to use the weapons correctly, the real victory is seen.

PRAYER

Father God, show us in your Word the value of this armor in Ephesians 6. Keep us ever conscious of this gift of spiritual equipping for living out our days on earth. Remind us of each piece of armor, as well as how and when to use it against the true enemy, satan. Help us to clearly distinguish between our fleshly desires (which we are to master) and the sin that can so easily create a fall in our lives. May we use this armor to protect our minds, bodies, and hearts. As we go about our days, help us to use each tool to the best of our ability, giving glory and honor to You in our lives. I ask this in Jesus' name. Amen.

DAY 5

— OUR FRUIT OF STANDING —

THE LAST STAND

The more Scripture you store in your heart, the longer you can keep standing, the more rapidly you can recognize deception, and the easier you can discern the spirit of a thing. As you pray God's Word, that Word will strengthen you, and your standing will become easier. Praying and knowing the Scripture will keep us strong as Christians. Prayer keeps doors shut that otherwise would be opened from a prayer-less life or an unprepared lifestyle. Prayer is the last item of spiritual armor and equipping that was detailed in our Bible passages from yesterday, in Ephesians 6:18:

> Praying always with all prayer and supplication
> in the Spirit, being watchful to this end with all
> perseverance and supplication for all the saints.

There is coming a last stand in front of the King of Kings and Lord of Lords. There is a real enemy out to get us; in battle terms, we are in his spiritual cross-hairs. Hollywood and others often imagine this to look like the final gun battle in many familiar old Western movies, but it will not be us wielding the guns in this fight! God has already made a way of escape for those who live for and trust Him.

> For I know that my redeemer liveth, and that He shall stand at the latter day upon the earth. (Job 19:25 KJV)

> And I saw the dead, small and great, standing before God, and books were opened. And another book was opened, which is the Book of Life. And the dead were judged according to their works, by the things which were written in the books. (Revelation 20:12)

Because the Blood of Jesus marks us, the enemy knows that if we learn the power of our weapons and use them, he is powerless against us. Our spiritual equipping in Jesus already rendered the enemy defeated; we remind him of that defeat—and our victory—each time we employ our God-given weapons against him. We, as the Church of Christ, must gain this same understanding! Our spiritual equippings are for us to use while we are still here on earth. God calls us to stand in the provision secured at the Cross by Jesus. It is His provision for our daily living and sustenance.

PRAYER

Father, thank you for each weapon You have proved to your children. I ask for wisdom and understanding in the use of each tool and that we become excellent warriors in this last stand against the enemy. Help us to see and know in each moment who our enemy is when we are going into battle to defend what You, Lord, have given so freely at such a precious cost to You. Teach us to use the Word of God, the truth in Your wisdom, our standing of righteousness, and the name above all other names, Jesus, in our fight of defense. Keep at the forefront of our minds that our battle isn't to win, as Jesus has already provided our win, but to disenable the enemy from using his tricks and lies against us and between us. I pray that as we put our armor on each day, we will walk in Your glory because of this beautiful gift of standing firm in Jesus. I ask this in the name of Jesus, amen.

DAY 6

— OUR FRUIT OF AUTHORITY —

SPEAKING OUR AUTHORITY

In Jesus' teaching during the Passover meal, He was preparing the disciples for a time of separation from Him. His words empowered them to live by faith victoriously even after He ascended. The authority of the believer is what He was leaving with them.

Jesus also taught them about the works or devices of their enemy, satan. Then, he taught them by whose authority He was sent and by whose authority He was speaking. He was teaching the authority of the believer to them and us.

> He has blinded their eyes and hardened their hearts, Lest they should see with their eyes, lest they should understand with their hearts and turn, so that I should heal them. (John 12:40)

> For I have not spoken on My own authority; but the Father who sent Me gave Me a command, what I should say and what I should speak. And I know that His command is everlasting life. Therefore, whatever I speak, just as the Father has told Me, so I speak. (John 12:49-50)

Many passages in the Bible instruct us to speak God's Word to our circumstances and sickness. Just like Jesus, this is how we activate our authority as believers; we declare it as a command based on the authority we have been given in Christ Jesus. Even though the Scriptures make a firm statement of the power of speaking God's Word, there are still many who do not understand this concept of authority because it hasn't been taught in many denominational churches.

I am aware that some might call this the "name it and claim it" doctrine. My encouragement to readers here is to take another look at the Word. Forget the traditions of men or what you have heard people say. Ask yourself, "What does the Word of God say?" These are Jesus' very own words, spoken from His mouth in the authority of the Father. My warning is to take caution when you decide to mock or accuse something of not being biblical. Although meant to be derogatory, 'name it and claim it,' as many call it, is clearly in the Bible. It only becomes unbiblical and fruitless when whatever we are naming and claiming is not based on God's instruction or in the will of God.

Other important things to consider: When and to whom did Jesus speak this vital message? It should be noticed that (in the verses listed above) Jesus was teaching his disciples about how things are to be done during Passover. Passover would be the time of the year just before He was to leave His disciples. We might understand the purpose and the practice better if we think of the conversations in this way:

Let's say you are planning to leave for a trip out of town or even for work each day. You might leave your loved ones with instructions for use while you are gone. Perhaps you will say, "Don't forget to feed the dog." Or, "Grandma is coming by to get you at 4 pm." One of the more famous instructions in our family has been, "Dinner is in the freezer. Just pop it in the microwave for 5 minutes. I love you; see you this afternoon." Then, we are off to our destination. Why do we do this? First, because the last thing we say is what we want them to remember most. Second, we know that it will help things go smoothly during the separation period, however long that may be.

Essentially, Jesus was preparing them for how to continue His work while He was gone. He knew we would need the help from above. We access the help Jesus lovingly provided for us through the leading of His Spirit, The Helper, and by using our authority in the name of Jesus. He knew we would need this for many reasons. His provision is purposeful, not something to be made fun of or misused. This authority of the believer He left with us is powerful, and God meant for it to be.

PRAYER

Father, teach us about the authority we have in the name of Jesus, the authority you left in the hands of every believer while we wait for your return. Teach us how valuable it is for our everyday lives. Help us to learn how to use Your mighty name properly and not just fling it here and there in every desired whim, disregarding its power. Teach us to honor your provisions and blessings and for them to bless our lives, giving you glory for all our circumstances. I pray this in the name of Jesus. Amen.

DAY 7

— OUR FRUIT OF PEACE —

JESUS AS OUR PEACE

Peace arrived on the earth the moment Jesus was born. Jesus is God's peace, finally establishing itself on earth. We, through salvation, are partakers of His peace; it's in us and goes with us.

Therefore, having been justified by faith, we have peace with God through our Lord Jesus Christ. (Romans 5:1)

Glory to God in the highest, and on earth peace, goodwill toward men! (Luke 2:14)

For it pleased the Father that in Him all the fullness should dwell, and by Him to reconcile all things to Himself, by Him, whether things on earth or things in heaven, having made peace through the blood of His Cross. (Colossians 1:19–20)

These Scriptures tell us that we have peace *with God*, and we have the peace *of God*. Jesus said,

> *"Peace I leave with you, My peace I give to you;* not as the world gives do I give to you. Let not your heart be troubled, neither let it be afraid" (John 14:27; emphasis added).

When I have received Christ as my Savior (as my Lord through the confession of my faith in Jesus), I have been given and have direct access to the peace of God. I have Jesus. He is mine, and I am His. As a joint heir with Christ, all that He has is mine. So, His peace is our peace!

> Now the fruit of righteousness is sown in peace by those who make peace. (James 3:18)

Salvation came through sacrifice, as well as peace. As we study peace in this chapter, remember not to take peace lightly. Peace and living in peace in America were established by the shedding of the blood of soldiers who fought in the past wars for it. God's peace was also established by the birth of Jesus and the shedding of Jesus' blood on the Cross. Peace is a gift, and God's peace is one of the most valuable assets a Christian has for life. Protect your peace, guard your peace, and if at all possible, choose peace in every situation.

PRAYER

Father, thank You for sending Your Son Jesus, Our Prince of Peace. May we understand what a profound cost this was for You and Him. Help us to choose peace today. Even where we could be tempted to desire vindication, allow us to remember the more excellent way of Life and living. In the name of Jesus, we pray. Amen.

DAY 8

— OUR FRUIT OF PEACE —

PEACE WITH OUR PHYSICAL BODIES

The Bible refers to a temple as a house; it also refers to *our bodies* as temples or houses. After Jesus' resurrection, His *house* or body was even more significant than it was in its former state.

> "The glory of this latter *temple* shall be greater than the former," says the Lord of hosts. "And in this place I will give peace," says the Lord of hosts. (Haggai 2:9; emphasis added)

> "The glory of this latter *house* shall be greater than the former," says the Lord of hosts: "and in this place will I give peace," saith the Lord of hosts. (Haggai 2:9 KJV; emphasis added)

What? Know ye not that *your body is the temple* of the Holy Ghost which is in you, which ye have of God, and ye are not your own? (1 Corinthians 6:19 KJV; emphasis added)

Jesus also referred to rebuilding the temple in three days in John 2:19, "Jesus answered and said to them, 'Destroy this temple, and in three days I will raise it up.'" Our bodies are precious to God. *We house the Spirit of God inside our bodies.* We are to care for and love our bodies because we are chosen vessels, a host for The Lord of Hosts!

Personally, it was a real struggle for me to be at peace with my body. I didn't make the connection of it being a holy, sacred place, a temple for the Lord, until many years after my salvation. Like so many others, I had abused my temple, intentionally in some ways and unintentionally in others, through ignorance mainly. For example, I gave it the wrong food, dangerous substances, or negative, murderous "talking to's" on too many occasions when I was angry.

In past times, when my husband had overheard me speaking about my body, he would get upset and tell me to stop saying those things about myself. He would tell me that my words were not Truth. In those seasons, I was aggressive in self-hatred. But the Word and my husband's words were working in me to deliver me from that self-hatred.

I began to see my surrender to salvation in Christ included the surrender of my temple to God. It wasn't until I stepped back from my disregard for my physical body and my own opinions that any true peace was able to exist. Until I chose to believe that I am a temple of the Holy Spirit, I could not experience all the peace that Jesus Christ died to redeem. But as I did, I began to see myself in a new way—as the Holy Spirit's dwelling place—and real change began to happen.

I am mostly at peace with my body today, but it continues to be a real work in progress. I am now, from glory to glory, experiencing peace and contentment in the gift of my body while dealing with the physical repairs I must fix from its previous abuse. It's a daily work to bring it closer to the ideal: *us* living *as* Jesus. This truth is in 1 John 4:17, "Love has been perfected among us in this: that we may have boldness in the day of judgment; because ***as He is, so are we*** in this world." In Christ, as He is, so am I in this world!

PRAYER

Father, I pray that by the revelation of Your Word, we will settle this issue of valuing and loving our bodies. By your equipping grace, let us see ourselves as the vessels carrying your Spirit in this earth. I pray that we receive your healing peace by making a choice today and every day to believe Your Word. Instill in us, your children, Lord, that we can have peace through Christ in our bodies as well as our minds, souls, and spirits. May we increase the care and love we release toward our bodies day by day. May we reverence and honor the sacrifice of the body of your Son, Jesus, and may we experience the peace you so graciously provided. I ask this in the name of Jesus. Amen.

DAY 9

— OUR FRUIT OF PEACE —

PEACE IN OUR ENVIRONMENT

Most would agree that there are many things, people, and places in the world around us that are not at all peaceful. Nevertheless, as Christians, our environment should never be the dictator of our internal peace. Did you know that we uniquely have the power to bring peace into any environment because Jesus' peace dwells in us? But to do so, we must first allow His supernatural, undefinable peace to rule in our hearts. We must establish this steady flow of peace within us before our external environments can feel the effects of this beautiful gift.

> And if the house be worthy, let your peace come upon it: but if it be not worthy, let your peace return to you. (Matthew 10:13 KJV)

According to this Scripture, I have recently begun to enter a building and say, "Peace to this house." By speaking this verse in faith, I have intentionally started allowing his peace to flow through me wherever I am. And do you know what? As I have done this, I have observed that while I am there, peace is there! Not because I am lovely and excellent at giving peace, but because of Him who is truly wonderful (or full of wonder) and awesome *in me.*

I have been told many times when someone is visiting my home, "There is so much peace here," or "Your house is so peaceful." It doesn't get that way because of who I am in the natural sense. It is peaceful because I purposefully allow His peace to have a place there. I will admit it is not always easy. I must fight the good fight of faith if I want to keep that peace so prevalent in my home.

The world houses and fosters an environment full of things that are the opposite of peace. We must be intentional in keeping our home a *habitat of peace.* To make sure our home is a refuge of peace, we must foster an atmosphere that is a source of rest from the environments we encounter out in the world all day at jobs and appointments.

> Blessed are the peacemakers, For they shall be called sons of God. (Matthew 5:9)

For example, we don't allow certain things into our house that would bring division, fear, or anxiety. We don't allow people to bring division into our environment. We don't have the news blaring out of the television all of the time. We don't watch movies that promote fear or sin (adultery, murder, people living together, etc.)

Jesus honors our faith when we make a place for His habitation. I encourage you to honor and make space for His gift of peace today and experience His peace in your environment.

PRAYER

Father, teach us ways to eliminate strife and stress. Grace us, Lord, to keep a habitat of peace in our homes and show us how to release your peace intentionally wherever you send us. Your peace is a precious gift that you have generously given to us. Help us find the best ways to employ and deploy your peace today. I ask this in the name of Jesus. Amen.

DAY 10

— OUR FRUIT OF PEACE —

PEACE IN ACTION AND AS OUR RESPONSE

You may have heard before or read in Galatians 5:22–23 that peace is one of the fruits of the Holy Spirit. For those who haven't, and as a reminder to all of us, I have included the verse below to read as we begin our devotional today:

> But the fruit of the Spirit is love, joy, peace, longsuffering, kindness, goodness, faithfulness, gentleness, self-control. Against such there is no law. (Galatians 5:22–23)

With that as a foundation, let's look at how we can more actively exhibit peace in our lives. In 2 Timothy 2:22, the Bible tells us to "flee also youthful lusts; but pursue righteousness, faith, love, peace with those who call on the Lord out of a pure heart." So we see that the Bible speaks of things and behaviors to avoid, but it also instructs us to *choose peace deliberately*.

Let's consider James 3:17–18 as our primary passage of Scripture for today:

> But the wisdom that is from above is first pure, then peaceable, gentle, willing to yield, full of mercy and good fruits, without partiality and without hypocrisy. Now the fruit of righteousness is sown in peace by those who make peace.

The passage helps us to dig in a little deeper. Just prior to this, in verse 16, it says, "for where envy and self-seeking exist, confusion and every evil thing are there." Then, of course, we can see that the Scripture goes on to give a list of good fruits, and that list includes peace. The last line of our passage tells us that "the fruit of righteousness is *sown in peace* by those who *make peace*" (emphasis added).

When our priorities are mercy, righteous living, and honesty, and when we emphasize pureness in our private lives, peace is the result. *Peace becomes the signature of our outward responses and actions.* These results are not separate from the priorities. They are our confident expectation. It's a promise from Jesus' work on the Cross. There is no way we can act or respond in peace to others or behave peacefully in a dire situation outside of the work of the Cross. Jesus endured the unfathomable pain of death on the Cross to provide us with His peace—the peace He brought with Him at His birth.

Peace isn't having enough *stuff* when things get tough in life. *Peace is the calm assurance that God will provide for all your needs.* In spite of any material thing that might be perceived as lacking in life, He is faithful to provide for His children.

Jesus' peace is faithful. However, a person can absolutely live a peaceless life as a Christian. I see it much more often than it needs to be. We must choose to walk in his peace. There is a give and take. For true peace to flow, not only in our lives and for our benefit but to let peace flow through us for others to experience as well, we must choose those actions that allow it to do so. This abiding peace is what gives glory to God.

PRAYER

Father, help us today to notice the areas of our lives that need the barber of Jesus' provision to cut the dead ends of attitudes or beliefs that split His intentions for our lives. Cut the dead ends that interrupt the flow of peace in our lives today. Trim our blind spots and bring attention to the planks in our view so we can experience the true precious peace in the way we react and act day to day. Thank you for your faithful, gentle pruning process that takes us from glory to glory. Remind us that just as we must be still while getting our hair trimmed, we must also be still while you are pruning our lives for the best results. I ask this of you in Jesus' name. Amen.

DAY 11

— OUR FRUIT OF PEACE —

WE ARE AT PEACE WITH GOD

Let's end this study on *Our Fruit of Peace* with the understanding that God isn't mad at us. Romans 5 says if we are in Jesus Christ, God is actually at peace with us. That is excellent news!

> Therefore, having been justified by faith, we have peace with God through our Lord Jesus Christ, through whom also we have access by faith into this grace in which we stand, and rejoice in hope of the glory of God. (Romans 5:1–2)

Romans is such an excellent book for finding our place in the Kingdom. He sent Jesus to redeem the peace between His creation and Himself. God makes it so simple by His pure love. It is made simple because we either choose to receive the gift of salvation and peace with God or we decide not to receive it. If we don't accept the gift, we commit the unforgivable sin of blasphemy as a rejection of God's gift of salvation. God left that choice up to us.

Earthly fathers are not always people we are at peace with. That connection could, in some new believers, leave a distaste in their mouth for God as Father because of how our earthly dads treated us or neglected us. For example, I don't have a good relationship with my earthly father. God, however, took over that job for him and showed me what a father looks like, how a father responds, and what the love of a father can feel like. It is a priceless relationship that took some brave moves on my part to move closer to God despite a failed relationship with my earthly father. The Lord invites us all to partake of the Father-child relationship with God despite the tainted images of fathers or fatherhood that the enemy may have placed into some of our lives; moving toward God as Father is well worth the effort.

What naturally followed from gaining a relationship with God? I was able to see the relationship with my earthly father that God intended us to have all along. Grace toward my earthly father grew out of a relationship with my Father God. Because of my relationship with Father God, I have an understanding of my natural father's struggles and mistakes. I came to realize that most of my father's struggles and mistakes are the same as those of many fathers. I came to understand that deception provides too many fathers with opportunities for failure; our earthly dads are *not* perfect but human, whereas Father God *is* perfect and *not* human. You can trust God. God is a perfect Father, full of love and peace for all who claim Him.

PRAYER

Thank you, Father God, for fostering truth in the hurt little child in me; thank you that you found this one who so desperately needed to know the truth of Father's love. I ask that You bring grace to me, to all of us, so that we can set aside the misguided hurts and painful moments of our earthly fathers and receive the truth of faithful Fatherhood only You can provide. Clean up the dysfunctions of our hearts that fallible men have shaped, who themselves had been previously deceived and scarred. Heal us all, kids and dads, in Your unique way, through the Father's peace in us—may we know you in a new way. I ask this in the name of Jesus. Amen.

DAY 12

— OUR FRUIT OF JOY —

JOY COMES

In our Christian walk, there are times when emotions run high or low. However, true joy and the fruit of the Spirit (including joy) are not feeling-based emotions. Those examples of joy are pure expressions of the very nature of God. He offers us the chance to house this joy within ourselves through the redemptive, reconciling power of salvation. This joy comes to us and is available to us via our spirit man and not by our soulish realm (the mind, will, and emotions).

> For His anger is but for a moment, His favor is for life; Weeping may endure for a night, But *joy* comes in the morning. (Psalm 30:5; emphasis added)

The word *joy* in Psalm 30:5 is from the Hebrew *rinnah* [pronounced "ree-nah"], and it means a shout of rejoicing, shouting, loud cheering in triumph, and singing.[6] *Rinnah* describes the joyful shouting at the time of a great victory, like the scripture below:

> When it goes well with the righteous, the city rejoices; and when the wicked perish, there is jubilation. (Proverbs 11:10)

This verse describes the jubilation of the righteous not just when the wicked are eliminated but also when it goes well with the righteous. God tells us that this is the benefit of having even just one righteous person in your city!

> You will show me the path of life; in Your presence is fullness of joy; at Your right hand are pleasures forevermore. (Psalm 16:11)

Joy, like love or longsuffering, is always available in our spirit through God's Holy Spirit. Our position in Christ has perfected it. When we accept Jesus Christ as Lord and Savior, we receive His love and the joy of the Lord. This joy does not come as a result of any circumstance outside of Him, nor the mood we happen to wake up in on any given morning! God's joy is like His promises—these are like little presents preciously wrapped for our seeking out and finding in Him.

A great thing about joy and the other fruits is that they are fully available to everyone who chooses to seek them out and put them on as a Christian. Joy comes when we press in and keep our faith in God. Peace comes not because our trials or challenging situations are finally over but because the peace that comes from God is available to us right in the middle of any trial, even as we walk it out! Joy is a lot like that type of peace. Joy in the midst of the storm is ours because God provides His peace to us daily.

PRAYER

Father, thank you for the joys we experience while we live in you. Thank you for the saturation of joy permeating our cities, which comes from knowing and living with You. Keep our minds set on the fullness of your joy today. Help us to touch others with this joy to give you the glory for our work victories, our victories in rest and recreation, and abiding victory in the day-in and day-out duties of our everyday lives. Amen.

DAY 13

— OUR FRUIT OF JOY —

JOY IN THE LORD

Christians experience unique and mighty hope because of their relationship with God. Our hope in Him and our ever-present joy can be experienced during any season of life if we release challenges from our hands and lay them in the mighty, power-filled hands of God.

> His Lord said to him, "Well done, good and faithful servant; you were faithful over a few things, I will make you ruler over many things. *Enter into the joy of your lord.*" (Matthew 25:21; emphasis added)

While I was with them in the world, I kept them in Your name. Those whom You gave Me

I have kept; and none of them is lost except the son of perdition, that the Scripture might be fulfilled. But now I come to You, and these things I speak in the world, that *they may have My joy fulfilled in themselves.* (John 17:12–13; emphasis added)

Now may the God of hope *fill you with all joy* and peace in believing, that you may abound in hope by the power of the Holy Spirit. (Romans 15:13; emphasis added)

Great is my boldness of speech toward you, great is my boasting on your behalf. I am filled with comfort. I am *exceedingly joyful in all our tribulation.* (2 Corinthians 7:4; emphasis added)

I believe that we have everything we need *in Christ*. If we need healing, it's been provided in the work of Christ. The same is true of prosperity, salvation, and protection from the many attacks of the enemy. I can't tell you that we will never have a bad day or that we won't experience challenging situations. For sure, in this world, we can experience the most severe conditions, but *in Christ*, we don't have to lack the joy of the Lord while experiencing those things. He has a way out of them or through them to the other side—that should bring joy to our hearts in the midst of chaos and trial.

Many painful things have passed through my doors of opportunity, but the Lord was so faithful to me during each trial. We can't supersede hardships in life, but we do walk differently through them because of this joy, this joy in the Lord.

The Lord fills us with comfort and gives relief in severe times of tumult through this very joy that only comes from Him. We will always only find this joy by leaning into Him and allowing Him to fill us during the good days and, more importantly, during the dark days. Blessed be the Name of the Lord!

PRAYER

Father, you are where I gain my strength; in you, I am strong from your joy in each situation I face. Thank you for your faithfulness in being right there to celebrate with me and to weep with me, knowing that our trials only last a short time. Your joy shines through the dark days to keep me. Help me to fully realize it's Your joy that will keep me strong in the times I am weak and to rely on You for strength when I have none. I am so thankful for Your joy. I am grateful You keep that joy alive in me. Amen

DAY 14

— OUR FRUIT OF JOY —

JOY IN WORSHIP

These daily devotions on *Our Fruit of Joy* are tools to help us cultivate a heart of joy in worship. But like most things in our spiritual walk, that joy is developed first in private times of worship long before it can be seen in a life of public worship. A fundamental principle of *joy in worship,* no matter if it is private or public, is the understanding that we worship to express our heart *for God.* Worship should never be about impressing other people.

> Make a joyful shout to the Lord, all you lands! Serve the Lord with gladness; come before His presence with *singing.* (Psalm 100:1–2; emphasis added)

Shout joyfully to the LORD, all the earth;
Break forth in song, *rejoice*, and sing praises.
Sing to the LORD with the harp, With the
harp and the sound of a psalm, With trumpets
and the sound of a horn; Shout joyfully before
the LORD, the King. (Psalm 98:4–6; emphasis
added)

As we look at having *joy in worship* in the Scriptures, we
find very similar Hebrew words for *singing* (Strong's H7445 -
rᵊnânâ)[7] and for the word *rejoice* (Strong's H7442 – rānan[8]) in
the passages from Psalm 98: 4–6. Both are defined as *to sing out
(for joy) with a ringing cry or a shout (for joy)*.

Today, we find in the Word that Jesus taught worship as an
internal place rather than an external location or public display:

Jesus said to her, "Woman, believe Me, the
hour is coming when you will neither on this
mountain, nor in Jerusalem, worship the Father. (John 4:21)

Having an open door to pray and exalt God at any moment is a magnificent benefit of serving God. Christians get
the opportunity to worship God in song, in deeds, in giving,
and in thanksgiving anywhere our life leads us.

One of the best ways to worship God, however, is in the
manner in which we live out every day at home with our family—when no one else is watching. That private life is a true

test of our worship. Our public lives, work lives, and really every area of our lives can be expressions of our worship, but let's remember that the key there would be to show, not merely tell, how Jesus has changed our lives! What we do matters more than who sees us and who doesn't.

Ministering to our people at home is by far more critical than what we produce for others to see in public. If you can get this right at home, it only becomes natural to continue genuine worship of God when out in the world.

Have you ever heard the saying, "worth their salt?" I believe the seasoning of our lives—our salt—first comes from how we live and worship at home. If our salt is to preserve those around us, it must be developed and used first in our own house, and this includes expressing a joyful demeanor for everyone else to experience. The goal is to *make life tasty* so that others will want to "taste and see that the Lord is good" (Psalm 34:8).

Similarly, our worship *in spirit and truth* happens *in the heart first* before a Christian can exhibit a surrendered life toward other people.

> But the hour is coming, and now is, when the true worshipers will worship the Father in spirit and truth; for the Father is seeking such to worship Him. God is Spirit, and those who worship Him must worship in spirit and truth. (John 4:23–24)

We must surrender to Him one to One first. Truth always births in our hearts before it can filter out to our hands. Worship works the same way. We should cultivate the desire to be more accountable to ourselves about the way worship shows up in our lifestyles. If you feel worship could be a more significant part of what you do and express daily, be specific and adamant about incorporating it in a greater dimension each day.

PRAYER

Father, teach us how to worship joyfully. Teach us that joy is a result of true worship. Give us an understanding of how the two are joined in such a strategic way. I thank You for hearing and receiving my worship and for letting me know that You enjoy my worship toward You. I marvel that this is one gift I can give to the God who has everything or could acquire anything without me. It is my gift to You through free will. It is an honor to be able to give my worship daily. If there are areas of my life where I could be more joyful or more worshipful, I ask that it be shown to me, and I can then move into a fully established relationship with You through worship. I ask this in the name of Jesus. Amen.

DAY 15

— OUR FRUIT OF JOY —

JOY AS A RESULT OF SALVATION

Salvation is a glorious miracle. It is the best of all miracles anyone can experience. It is complete and whole-bodied; it is eternal and true; it is firm and cannot be lightly disposed of. It is permanent as long as we do not turn away from God.

Beloved, do not think it strange concerning the fiery trial which is to try you, as though some strange thing happened to you; but rejoice to the extent that you partake of Christ's sufferings, that when His glory is revealed, you may also be glad with exceeding joy. (1 Peter 4:12–13)

You have multiplied the nation and increased its joy; they rejoice before You according to the joy of harvest, as men rejoice when they divide the spoil. (Isaiah 9:3)

Therefore with joy you will draw water from the wells of salvation. (Isaiah 12:3)

Instead of your shame you shall have double honor, and instead of confusion they shall rejoice in their portion. Therefore in their land they shall possess double; everlasting joy shall be theirs. (Isaiah 61:7)

Therefore thus says the Lord God: behold my servants shall not eat, but you shall be hungry. Behold my servants shall drink, but you shall be thirsty; behold, my servants shall rejoice, but you shall be ashamed; behold, my servants shall sing for joy oh heart, but you shall cry for sorrow of heart and wail for grief of spirit. (Isaiah 65:13–14)

I have no greater joy than to hear that my children walk in truth. (3 John 4)

Salvation is a complete healing, restoration, new life, and prosperous gift. Salvation is each of those things and more wrapped up in one simple yet vital decision. If you can answer "*yes*" to the questions below, if you can surrender yourself to Him for eternity, salvation is yours to receive today:

> Do I accept what Jesus did on the Cross for me and suspend all my plans to live the way He has asked me to live?

> Do I serve only Him the rest of my life, to be obedient to His Word and to the way it teaches me to live every day?

> Do I believe Jesus came in the flesh and died on the Cross for the redemption of my sins?

> Can I love Him and make Him my priority for the rest of my days?

I can still remember the day I received salvation. It happened several times as I was growing up, and I like to say I was saved 157 times from age 6 to 22. But then there comes a specific time, a set time when you realize and surrender entirely and fully embrace His way of living.

This moment came for me at the age of 32. Even though I knew I was *saved* for many years before that, I surrendered *my will* at the age of 32. I was in a church that I would not usually have attended. But this day, my husband wanted to go there. I'm so thankful that he did! Because it was that day that I said, "You win, Lord, You win all of me."

When I walked out to our car, I looked around, and everything in this natural world seemed so extraordinary and new. The grass was greener and fresher, the air was lighter, the sun was brighter, and there was an added beauty to everything I could see. This phenomenon of supernatural beauty and brightness continued during the entire drive home that day. I knew I was different, not just saved, but *changed*.

The joy in that experience cannot be adequately described; it can only be fully experienced. I knew I was redeemed, and I had so much hope, joy, and love. Oddly enough, I even had an appreciation for the country music that was playing on the radio during the drive home! I have never enjoyed country music (and I still basically don't, but I respect it), but that day, I found joy in even country music!

PRAYER

Father, of all the things that You offer to us, Your salvation is the best, most fulfilling gift for life. Thank You for Your gift of salvation, the work of a loving, giving, and fierce force of a Father's love. I wish I had experienced it so much earlier in life than I did, but I am so glad You found me when You did. I am forever grateful for the saving of my life and all that it means to have this pure, unfiltered connection between the two of us. You are in me; I am in Christ; Christ is in me. Life is perfect that way. Thank you for such a wonderful life here on earth, and I know my eternity with You will be so much more than I can imagine. I pray You and I together can reach them all,

Lord, to bring them all into the knowing and understanding of who You really are. I love you, Father God; I love Jesus and the Holy Spirit. I pray we all come to know and have a relationship with You. In the name of Jesus, I pray this. Amen.

DAY 16

— OUR FRUIT OF JOY —

JOY IN THE WORD

We have discovered in previous days that joy is connected to our worship, is a result of our salvation, and is a reflection of our abiding in Christ and the peace of God. Joy is also cultivated by time spent in the Word of God. Yes, there is joy in the Word! We experience joy as a result of meditating on God's Word, singing His Word, or speaking His Word out loud. Each way of expression is beneficial for our spirit and body, but did you know that they also fill the space, the atmosphere, in the room around us with joy and peace as we speak or sing God's Word?

> These things I have spoken to you, *that My joy may remain in you, and that your joy may be full.* (John 15:11; emphasis added)

71

The Word of God inside us brings us joy. We hear this Word through reading our Bibles in individual study time or group Bible studies, through listening to sermons, and even by hearing from the Lord Himself by the Holy Spirit.

Now, I know that lots of people say that you can't trust people who say they hear from God, but I tell you this: I am very suspicious of anyone who can't hear the voice of God deep in their spirit-man, in their heart. The truth is that God speaks to us all the time; we just have to tune our ears to His precious voice. One of the main reasons Jesus went to the Cross was to redeem us and restore our relationship with the Father! That includes the restoration of the two-way conversation between God and his children.

If hearing the voice of God through His Word and his Holy Spirit is foreign to you or unfamiliar, here is a natural example to help illustrate why it is essential. What if I never heard anything my husband said to me? Yes, it would be a silent house, but more than that, it would also make for a very lonely existence and a strained relationship.

Communication in both directions is vital for long-term relationships. Once communication is gummed up or ceases, so does the relationship. Our relationship with God is no different than any human relationship here on earth in that they both require two-way conversations. Conversations bring us joy in the ability to hear the other's voice and to connect with them through understanding.

God's Word is living, and when we receive it inside us, that Word produces life and joy. Abiding in Him, in His Word, is key to actively receiving the joy of the Lord. We began our devotional today with a verse from John chapter 15. This chapter of the Gospel of John is all about how we are to abide in Christ, and it teaches us this using a very natural example of a fruit vine. Jesus said,

I am the true vine, and My Father is the vinedresser. Every branch in Me that does not bear fruit He takes away; and every branch that bears fruit He prunes, that it may bear more fruit. You are already clean because of the word which I have spoken to you. Abide in Me, and I in you. As the branch cannot bear fruit of itself, unless it abides in the vine, neither can you, unless you abide in Me.

I am the vine, you are the branches. He who abides in Me, and I in him, bears much fruit; for without Me you can do nothing. If anyone does not abide in Me, he is cast out as a branch and is withered; and they gather them and throw them into the fire, and they are burned. If you abide in Me, and My words abide in you, you will ask what you desire, and it shall be done for you. By this My Father is glorified, that you bear much fruit; so you will be My disciples.

As the Father loved Me, I also have loved you; abide in My love. If you keep My commandments, you will abide in My love, just as I have kept My Father's commandments and abide in His love.

These things I have spoken to you, that My joy may remain in you, and that your joy may be full. (John 15:1–11)

What do we do with the fruit of a natural vine? We consume it for fuel and nutrition. It brings life to our bodies. In much the same way that grapes produce juice and wine for nourishment when pressed, God's Word produces joy, which is nourishment (strength) to our spirit, soul, and body. The Word of God that we consume (hear, receive, and meditate on) dwells in us and provides nourishment to our spirit-man, renewal to our mind, and healing to our natural bodies.

The incorruptible Word of God is a deafening weapon to the corruptible world we live in. It will silence the pain and disease so that we can live in daily victory. I encourage you today to make it a point to add the joyful noise of God's Word into your atmosphere. You have the power to recreate your atmosphere by finding joy in the Word and releasing shouts of praise from your mouth.

PRAYER

Father God, teach us to abide in Your Word, the resource for life and joy. May your Word give pure credit to Jesus's finished work, which was completed in Him and is also now complete in us. Establish in us the understanding of who you are and your desire for our lives. Cause your joy to remain in us to the full, as spoken in your Word. I ask these things in the name of Jesus Christ, amen.

DAY 17

— OUR FRUIT OF JOY —

COUNT IT ALL JOY

I don't know about you, but this one is rather difficult for me. I am learning to seek joy in situations quicker now, but the flesh part likes to have an opinion quite quickly. Initially, as I face a trial or test or bad news, I find it hard to find joy in it. But the Word tells me to do just that in spite of the way I see things happening.

> My brethren, count it all joy when you fall into various trials, knowing that the testing of your faith produces patience. (James 1:2–3)

This joy is not about how I feel about any given situation, but it is about *who* I am trusting to walk with me in this given situation! Thank goodness I don't have to rely only on myself to get myself through tough things. I can fully cast it over to my Savior, and He knows the best way to walk it out every single time. The Word of God contains powerful prayers like the one in Colossians 1:9–14 to assist us:

> For this reason we also, since the day we heard it, do not cease to pray for you, and to ask that you may be filled with the knowledge of His will in all wisdom and spiritual understanding;

> that you may walk worthy of the Lord, fully pleasing Him, being fruitful in every good work and increasing in the knowledge of God;

> strengthened with all might, according to His glorious power, for all patience and longsuffering with joy; giving thanks to the Father who has qualified us to be partakers of the inheritance of the saints in the light.

> He has delivered us from the power of darkness and conveyed us into the kingdom of the Son of His love, in whom we have redemption through His blood, the forgiveness of sins.

These Biblical prayers are effective in navigating the steps of our everyday lives. I can tell you that not once has the Word led me in the wrong direction. God can be trusted, and His

Word contains help for anything that comes at us and tries to defeat us. There—right there—is where the joy is found! It is waiting for you at the intersection of the Word and your trust in Him.

I admit, however, that for several years, I didn't like these verses. I thought to myself, "Why on earth would being joyful about trials be relevant for a Christian? Surely not!" After I decided to stop being offended by this verse and find out what I was missing in it, I learned there is great power in applying it, and I did not have that before.

If trials pop up, and they will, we can immediately have joy centered in God's absolute ability to guide us faithfully through the thorny path out to complete relief. He knows the way. It is up to us to surrender to His way.

People can choose to allow disease like cancer, or losing a job, or source of livelihood, or a most defeating trial of losing someone we love as being more powerful than the blood of Christ with its redemptive anointing for simple trust. That will leave every step up to us, and I have done it that way and failed. The other option is for a person to look any of those circumstances straight into their core, then turn to God and show their trust in Him for the outcome with joy and a knowing that He is faithful and sure to keep us.

Recently, we suddenly needed a new HVAC system for our house. We chose to take the viewpoint of how we *get* to change our old system for a better one. A fresh perspective brought joy in the trial, knowing our Lord was working for the best outcome of the situation because we had put our trust in Him.

He will perform good works. God will take care of His own in every circumstance. And He does it every time we put our trust in Him for it. The first step is always ours to make. He will not invade our situations to say, "Hey kid, step aside, I got you." No, but He will say that if we surrender our fears and questions to Him, depending on Him to direct our actions!

This passage of Scripture is now one of my favorite promises because I understand its depth and hope to learn even more about it as time goes on.

PRAYER

Oh, Father! Thank You for giving us the opportunity to choose joy over fear in our lives. Thank You for taking such great care of Your children. Help us to move quicker in Your direction of trust when the enemy shoots his arrows our way. Help us to learn to wholly lean into Your promises and faithful nature to guide our steps through each challenging situation, even the deadliest of situations. Fill us with Your joy while we wait for the good results You can administer in our situations of life. I trust You. I love You. I ask these things in the power-filled name of Jesus. Amen.

Day 18

— OUR FRUIT OF TRUST —

OUR CONFIDENCE OF TRUST

Trusting God is woven throughout the Bible. You can find the idea of trust in the Bible through a variety of words that describe the concept, such as *keep, secure, belief, conviction, faith*, and others. Our trust in God stabilizes our faith; you might connect the two words *faith* and *trust* with the thought that having trust in God *is* having true faith.

> But I have trusted in Your mercy; My heart shall rejoice in Your salvation. I will sing to the Lord, Because He has dealt bountifully with me. (Psalm 13:5–6)

Blessed is that man who makes the Lord his
trust, and does not respect the proud, nor such
as turn aside to lies. (Psalm 40:4)

The more I come to know Christ and who He is, and the
more firmly I grasp who I am in Him, a platform of trust is
established in me. As we grow in our knowledge of Christ, we
find that trusting in Christ produces a type of confidence in us
that does not exist in all things outside of Him.

For we are the circumcision, who worship God
in the Spirit, rejoice in Christ Jesus, and have
no confidence in the flesh. (Philippians 3:3)

This verse is very clear about what is not to be trusted,
which is the flesh. *Knowing what is not to be trusted only insures
us of what and who is to be trusted.* It's always good to be able to
mark off what is not so as to better see and focus on the truth
of what is.

Jesus Christ is the same yesterday, today, and
forever. (Hebrews 13:8)

This verse is such a beautiful picture of how confident we
can be in trusting Jesus, His values, His character, and His
Word. Think about someone you know personally and trust
without a lot of thought or evaluation. Are they also genuinely
consistent? Do they do the same thing excellently and faithfully

so often that you have learned that things placed in their hands will get done and finished well? We know this of them because they have always been the people to rely on over time, right?

A classic example for many might be the one who vacuums the fellowship hall after a church gathering! Most church members know who that person is. In fact, an image of them might have popped up in your mind just now. For you, it might be an image of another person you know that serves faithfully. However, the point is that those church members, friends, or coworkers are trustworthy because they consistently perform the job and are faithful to do so over time.

Each time I needed to trust Jesus in a delicate situation or even to just get me back home in the middle of a storm, it was natural, automatic, and easy to trust Him. Why? Because He has proven Himself faithful, and my heart knows that I can trust Him.

There is a unique blessing in the ability to trust Jesus above all worldly advice. There is a confidence that comes from trusting God for what I should do in my situation rather than believing every opinion floating around or reading through the millions of conflicting articles found on Internet searches! It honors Him when we trust Him and turn to God *first*. Every time I place my confidence in trusting God above how my flesh may feel about any given direction, that foundation of faith and trust in God grows stronger.

Whatever it is that may be heavy on your mind today, know Jesus is trustworthy and will move excellently in that situation. Lay it in His hands today and trust Him to provide the victory.

PRAYER

Father, forgive me for not trusting and relying on Jesus in every painful or overwhelming situation in my life. I surrender all the things I cannot do into Your hands. I trust you to do what only you can do and to equip me to do my part. I trust that Jesus can and will accomplish what is needed and handle all that is out of my control. Thank you, Father, for this confidence in your Son. Amen.

DAY 19

— OUR FRUIT OF TRUST —

OUR HERITAGE OF TRUST

For each of us, there are facts about our natural heritage that can be proven through DNA—many of those inherited traits we can see with our natural eyes. Did you know that beyond the facts of our natural heritage, there is an eternal heritage—a divine nature— activated in our lives when we are born-again through salvation in Jesus Christ? I cherish both but fully trust the latter.

> In Him also we have obtained an inheritance, being predestined according to the purpose of Him who works all things according to the counsel of His will, that we who first trusted in Christ should be to the praise of His glory. (Ephesians 1:11–12)

Our fathers trusted in You; They trusted, and You delivered them. They cried to You, and were delivered; They trusted in You, and were not ashamed. (Psalm 22:4–5)

For You are my hope, O Lord God; You are my trust from my youth. By You I have been upheld from birth; You are He who took me out of my mother's womb. My praise shall be continually of You. (Psalm 71:5–6)

Combining several sources, we can define *heritage*[9] as property that is or may be inherited; an inheritance; valued objects and qualities such as cultural traditions, unspoiled countryside, and historic buildings that have been passed down from previous generations; denoting a traditional brand or product regarded as emblematic of fine craftsmanship; a unique or individual possession; an allotted portion.[10]

So we see that our *heritage* is not only something that is in us from conception (naturally and spiritually) but also something tangible that can be passed down through generations. Both examples of a heritage are valuable. The heritage that comes through Christ makes us a part and partner in the Kingdom of God. This spiritual inheritance comes with the confidence of trust and proven value throughout centuries, being observable and experienced by many believers in Him. Psalm 121 speaks of the benefits of our heritage through Christ:

I will lift up my eyes to the hills—From whence comes my help? My help comes from the Lord, Who made heaven and earth.

He will not allow your foot to be moved; He who keeps you will not slumber. Behold, He who keeps Israel shall neither slumber nor sleep.

The Lord is your keeper; The Lord is your shade at your right hand. The sun shall not strike you by day, Nor the moon by night.

The Lord shall preserve you from all evil; He shall preserve your soul. The Lord shall preserve your going out and your coming in from this time forth, and even forevermore.

These verses in Psalm 121 are among the many throughout the Bible that remind me of our heritage of trust. Although I was born with a distinct natural heritage, I have also been born again with God's heritage and benefits. The heritage we have in the Word of God is there to equip us for practical application in everyday life. There is great hope and help in knowing His Word belongs to me, and it is compelling and true. God's Word is trustworthy, applicable, and proven time and time again.

PRAYER

Today, Father, assist me in seeing and understanding the full scope of this eternal inheritance portioned to me in Christ Jesus. Help me value its wealth and validity, guide me, and hold me fast to whatever comes my way here on earth. Knowing and understanding how I will one day experience it fully in its vastness, I trust you, Lord, with all the uncertainty of today.

Knowing You will keep me in perfect peace; as my mind stays on You, I trust you fully. Thank you for the priceless heritage of trusting, serving, and communing with You for all eternity. Amen.

DAY 20

— OUR FRUIT OF TRUST —

OUR PROMISE OF TRUST

Each of the passages below emphasizes a specific result of trusting God. As we start our devotional time today, I recommend that you read them out loud and look for the focus noted:

- Proverbs 3:5–6 Sleep and trust without fail

- Proverbs 16:20 Trust brings happiness

- Proverbs 28:25 Trust in God brings prosperity

- Psalm 28:7   Trust in God brings assistance

- Psalm 32:10   Trust brings mercy

- Psalm 84:12   Trust brings blessings

- Psalm 125:1 Trust brings stability

- 2 Corinthians 1:9–10 Trust brings salvation

These verses show me that I had to surrender myself and trust God to receive salvation, sleep, happiness, prosperity, and mercy. Psalm 37:3–8 also speaks to us about trusting God and the results He promises:

> Trust in the Lord, and do good; dwell in the land, and feed on His faithfulness.

> Delight yourself also in the Lord, and He shall give you the desires of your heart.

> Commit your way to the Lord, trust also in Him, and He shall bring it to pass.

> He shall bring forth your righteousness as the light, and your justice as the noon day.

> Rest in the Lord, and wait patiently for Him; do not fret because of him who prospers in his way. Because of the man who brings wicked schemes to pass.

Cease from anger, and forsake wrath; do not
fret – it only causes harm.

In past years, our family moved to another state because we
knew the Lord was leading us in that direction and to a particular church in that area. The verses in Psalm 37:3–8 were the
verses God used to encourage us as we followed His directions
and trusted Him in each decision.

It was indeed a walk of faith. Our things would need to be
stored during the move until appropriate housing was secured.
One load at a time, we packed and moved our belongings into
a storage unit in the new city. During this transition, neither
my husband nor I knew of any available jobs in the new state.
Every time we loaded up to take more of our stuff to the new
city, we would look for housing to move into.

As we continued on this journey of trusting in the promises
of God, we would try to have as many job interviews as possible with each trip to move a load of belongings. Establishing
a new job for my husband was our priority, and mine would
come with time. We knew this because I was only licensed to
work in the state we were moving from. Finding established
work for me would take longer.

The point here is that this transition wasn't determined by
job status or living arrangements. We knew God was faithful
and would show us the direction and the details for both of
those concerns. As we obeyed each simple direction from Him,
trusting in His leadership, we were able to quickly become es-

tablished and serve in our new (and still unfamiliar) church home.

Selling our house, delivering our letters of resignation, and then transporting our whole lives somewhere we've not been familiar with was both exciting and tense. We could have maybe moved a little slower, but we knew we had a purpose in that place called *there* and didn't want to miss out on any of it.

It was our trust in God during this three-month time that made this transition so fulfilling. It was filled with peace and full of God. We were never homeless or jobless. We were never hungry or needful of essential things. We also fit right in with the new church body—planted where God sent us—as if we had been there forever. This move would have never happened this smoothly if we didn't know how to trust God when we heard Him say, "Go *there*." Trust is the basis for receiving our promises from God.

PRAYER

Thank you for the guidance and wisdom provided to us when we learn to trust You, Lord. Teach us to trust You in all the little things every day so we don't question or falter when the larger requests come from your heart to ours or from our hearts to yours. May we continually exchange untethered levels of trust back and forth between us. We desire to be found trustworthy, that You are able to trust our obedience, as we continue to trust in You. By your equipping, may our promises to You be equally valid and sure as Your promises are to us. Amen.

DAY 21

— OUR FRUIT OF TRUST —

OUR TRUST IN GOD

Trusting God is a foundational duty as a Christian. Trusting Him is the basis for all that we pray, why we ask for things, and why we surrender our lives and future to Him in the process and act of salvation.

Our trust in God is more than just being thankful; it is an attitude or position in our hearts. Trusting is an active, almost physical act of movement into Him. Trust creates actual change, and yet it is something more challenging to release than thankfulness. Let's walk through some verses that speak of our trust in God:

> For to this end we both labor and suffer reproach, because we trust in the living God, who is the Savior of all men, especially of those

who believe. These things command and teach.
(1 Timothy 4:10–11)

Be angry, and do not sin. Meditate within your heart on your bed, and be still. Offer the sacrifices of righteousness, and put your trust in the Lord. (Psalm 4:4–5)

And those who know Your name will put their trust in You; for you, Lord, have not forsaken those who seek You. (Psalm 9:10)

For I will not trust in my bow, nor shall my sword save me. But You have saved us from our enemies, and have put to shame those who hated us. In God we boast all day long and praise Your name forever. Selah. (Psalm 44:6–8)

Whenever I am afraid, I will trust in You. In God (I will praise His word), In God I have put my trust; I will not fear. What can flesh do to me? (Psalm 56:3–4)

In God I have put my trust; I will not be afraid, what can man do to me? (Psalm 56:11)

He who dwells in the secret place of the Most High shall abide under the shadow of the Almighty. I will say of the Lord, "He is my refuge and my fortress; My God, in Him I will trust." (Psalm 91:1–2)

Thus says the Lord: "Cursed is the man who trust in man and makes flesh his strength, whose heart departs from the Lord. For he shall be like a shrub in the desert, and shall not see when good comes, but shall inhabit the parched places in the wilderness, in a salt land which is not inhabited. Blessed is the man who trusts in the Lord, and whose hope is the Lord. (Jeremiah 17:5–7)

It is a sage act (an act of wisdom) to trust God. The Scripture teaches us that we can trust God not only in our desperate moments of life but also in all the good and blessed things we acquire and endeavor to accomplish. We can trust Him with our spouses and children and with our jobs and our finances. God expects us to rely on His guidance and use wisdom–asking for wisdom that He gives liberally–to do what we can do in the natural. What we cannot do in the natural, we can know He will accomplish supernaturally.

Many times, it takes people quite a while to trust God. Typically, after many of our own failed attempts, we finally learn, or perhaps finally decide, to trust God with some things or someone precious to our hearts. As we come to know Him through the Word of God, we can come to the place where we understand with our whole heart that what is precious to us is most likely even more precious to Him. As we learn of His nature and character, we also come to know that God is well able to handle our precious treasures with great care and has even more excellent resources to choose what is best for us.

> Now to Him who is able to do exceedingly abundantly above all that we ask or think, according to the power that works in us! (Ephesians 3:20)

What often happens, however, is that we eventually *lend* Him certain things for a time. Maybe for some like me, the more minor things are more *comfortable* to lend to Him. Many times, giving things in my life over to Him would only happen after I have had my hands on them first. However, as we grow in grace and the Word, we discover that the sooner we relinquish our control of all things—in the beginning, before we mess anything up—the better the outcome will be!

Unfortunately, in the past, no matter how vital my trust in God was, it was too often my last resort. Like many, perhaps you, I had the mindset of handling everything myself until it failed or was unfruitful. Only then would I surrender it to God, saying, "Well, I guess now it's time to pray about it."

It is a greater faith to trust Him *first* and let Him seal the deal or land the transaction. The hardest lessons taught me that I am most blessed and less stressed when I lean into God *first*, not second, or as a last resort. Trust is learned. I can say that again. *Trust is learned.* As I said, these were some of the hardest lessons of my past.

Trust is a lesson that I take the time to communicate to you here to save you much heartache and delay. The best posture is one of trust, standing back to observe God's handwork from the start. I can tell you from experience that He always gives us the project back in much better condition than we could ever accomplish without him!

It pleases God that we enjoy the benefit of our faith in Him to complete the work He began. On the rare occasions when I have trusted God with something that He did not give back, in every instance, His actions have always proved to be what was best for me and my future. Lovingly, He knows all these things and desires His very best for us—which is an extra benefit of trusting Him.

PRAYER

Father, teach us gently to make your feet or your hands the first place we lay our earthly treasures. Keep our hearts supple in our surrender to You. Show me today the different areas of life in which I may be struggling to trust You. Forgive me for not understanding You thoroughly enough to run to You right away with the concerns and desires in my life. Forgive me when I forget You are the creator of all things, and You are before all things, and all things exist through You. Keep in the forefront of my decisions how I am complete only in You. Remind me, Lord, when I struggle, I am alive together with Christ, Your very own Son, making me an heir to all You have placed in Him. Just as You denied Him only once so that You would never again need to deny me, I can, therefore, fully trust You. I ask these things in the name of Jesus, my Savior. Amen.

DAY 22

— OUR FRUIT OF WORSHIP —

DAVID'S WORSHIP

When I think of worship, I think of King David. David understood worship before he was ever appointed King of Israel. He worshiped God in the field as he shepherded his family's livestock. No one was around most of the time during those long days with the flocks, so David had time to get to know who God was. He had the opportunity to prove God faithful when he fought bears or other predators coming after his flock. David worshiped God through the character of his heart before he ever danced publicly in his *skivvies* (that is Southern-speak for undergarments).

I will praise you, O Lord, with my whole heart;
I will tell of all Your marvelous works. I will

be glad and rejoice in You; I will sing praise to Your name, O Most High. (Psalm 9:1–2)

It is good to give thanks to the Lord, and to sing praises to Your name, O Most High; to declare Your lovingkindness in the morning, and Your faithfulness every night. (Psalm 92:1–2)

Every man worships something. The foundation of worship begins in deep places of one's character. Most of our character pre-salvation was basically searching to find anything to worship, be that self-promotion, success, talent, or lofty ideals promoting our careers or business or other things from the world around us.

When we come into Christ, that must change. God requires that He holds first place in our lives and that we have no other gods before him. The character of man, I believe, is fully transformed after salvation, and the new goal is to discover all the ways one can please God from a thankful heart. As the seed of worship takes root in our very being after salvation, the power of God in the Word of God waters that root and transforms the self-seeking and self-pleasing natural man into the God-seeking and God-pleasing worshiper.

What we are speaking of is an evolution from a carnal man who worships himself to a spiritual man who worships God. I have heard many teachers say there is no such thing as evolution and we shouldn't believe in it. I have a much different thought on that because I think what they could better say is that we should not believe in Darwin's Theory of Evolution, as God clearly has a concept of evolution, too! In the Bible, we are explicitly told to embrace evolution. It's in Romans 12:1–2:

> I beseech you therefore, brethren, by the mercies of God, that you present your bodies a living sacrifice, holy, acceptable to God, which is your reasonable service. And do not be conformed to this world, but be transformed by the renewing of your mind, that you may prove what is that good and acceptable and perfect will of God.

To be transformed speaks of evolution. Evolving into the image of Christ Himself is the acceptable and perfect will of God. God wills this to be in our lives. God created evolution as the transformation we experience through Salvation. Much of that transformation involves worship.

Don't let another day go by not being sure if you have evolved through salvation alone. Know that you know that you know you are a child of God. Worship is a great tool to use to switch the focus from self-worship to God-worship. It gets your mind off yourself and on Him and makes life all about Him.

> It is good to give thanks to the Lord, and to sing praises to Your name, O Most High. (Psalm 92:1)

Salvation and transformation will naturally implant this desire in new believers. It is our honor to continue our worship of God and to keep self-promotion at bay. Giving praise unto the Lord every day, in every situation, even in the middle of any heartache, can be one of the biggest blessings of our Christian walk.

PRAYER

Father, today, could you grant us a new view of David's heart in worship? May we praise only You through this understanding from Your Word all the days of our lives! Amen.

DAY 23

— OUR FRUIT OF WORSHIP —

THE MEDITATION OF MY HEART

The meditation of our spirit-man, what we feed our spirit, establishes the foundation for our worship of God and how securely we stay connected to His desires.

> Let the words of my mouth and the meditation of my heart be acceptable in Your sight, O Lord, my strength and my Redeemer. (Psalm 19:14)

That which we feed on, what we meditate on day and night, precedes our worship. Correct and balanced meditation of the Bible precedes the flow of correct, honorable worship. I desire to present excellent worship to God because He deserves no less. Worship is not about me, but it must always be about Him, to Him, and only for Him.

> Sing praises to God, sing praises! Sing praises to our King, sing praises! For God *is* the King of all the earth; Sing praises with understanding. (Psalm 47:6–7)

Worship in music and song is what comes to mind when most people think of worship. In truth, musical worship is a necessary yet much smaller part of the whole-life worship we offer Him. Worship happens every day, every week, and every year, in all the small details, too, not just in the song service on Sunday morning.

Worship is being diligent in showing up, wholly devoted, and present where we are supposed to be—like showing up when we are always the one called on to substitute as a teacher in the Sunday school class for 4- to 6-year-olds even when we believe it's not our calling. Worship is being at church every time you're able, even if you'd rather watch it from home live online because it's just easier.

Most importantly, worship is the position in which we keep our hearts as our eyes stay on God. Worship looks like the type of decisions we make at work, at home, and in our very private moments on any given day. Worship is being honest, even if it places you in a lower light from someone else's perspective. Worship is being a trusted, committed part of the Body of Christ while you shop for groceries at the local marketplace. Worship can even be sitting with other parents, ministering profound truths, during yet another baseball or soccer game this week.

PRAYER

Father, I am so thankful we have the opportunity and honor of worshiping You. I thank you for the Bible to use as a guide for understanding true worship. Keep our meditations and minds toward You as we read and study Your Word. Help us always to keep You at the center of our worship. Amen.

DAY 24

— OUR FRUIT OF WORSHIP —

SING UNTO THE LORD

I have stood next to believers in church services so many times who are intentionally worshiping God with a pure heart in or with their spiritual tongue. Those were genuinely blessed and edifying times, not because my earthly mind could understand the song they sang but because my eternal spirit could agree with the song of their spirit at that moment.

> For if I pray in an unknown tongue, my spirit prayeth, but my understanding is unfruitful.
>
> What is it then? I will pray with the spirit, and I will pray with the understanding also: I will sing with the spirit, and I will sing with the

understanding also. (1 Corinthians 14:14–15 KJV)

The passage above does not condemn a Christian if one doesn't pray or speak in tongues but instead gives the proper guidelines for this act as a demonstration. I believe in this gift of speaking, praying, and singing in tongues because the Bible says to. I intentionally purpose to pray, sing, and speak in the tongues of the Spirit, and I encourage others to do so as well. It is a part of the fruits of a Christian's life. It edifies and builds us up.

Praying and singing in the spirit with tongues is one of the highest forms of worship. I found that singing in tongues opens a connection like no other to God Himself. The Bible says our spirits speak truth, and God fully understands it as an excellent form of true worship. It edifies the Body, and it blesses God.

> Jesus said to her, "Woman, believe Me, the hour is coming when you will neither on this mountain, nor in Jerusalem, worship the Father. You worship what you do not know; we know what we worship, for salvation is of the Jews. But the hour is coming, and now is when the true worshipers will worship the Father in spirit and in truth, for the Father is seeking such to worship Him. God is Spirit, and those

who worship Him must worship in spirit and truth." (John 4:21–24)

PRAYER

Father, thank you for each gift of worship and each form of its expression. May You be blessed and enjoy each form of worship I give to You, as that is my goal. Worship is part of your will for us, and Your plan for our relationship with you is perfect. Help us to keep these gifts orderly and decently presented as we yield to the Holy Spirit and our love for You. Amen.

DAY 25

— OUR FRUIT OF WORSHIP —

WORSHIP THROUGH OBEDIENCE

I had to include my favorite scripture about worship in this week's lessons, and 1 Timothy 1:17 is that verse:

> Now to the King eternal, immortal, invisible,
> to God who alone is wise, be honor and glory
> forever and ever. Amen.

The verse above contains such beautiful speech when it says, "to the King eternal, immortal… who alone is wise." This language illustrates that God is set apart—above—all other things we might enjoy and love.

Taking that further, verse 18 of that same chapter teaches us that we are, like Timothy, charged to give honor and glory to God, saying, "This charge I commit to you, son Timothy, according to the prophecies previously made concerning you, that by them you may wage the good warfare (1 Timothy 1:18).

As we observed in yesterday's devotional, we have many ways to worship God. Obedience and honor go hand in hand and are among the ways we can worship God. In context, these verses show us that to obey God is to honor God; to honor God is a high form of worship.

When we obey something outside of God, we can actually be worshipping it through our obedience. For example, if someone has a stronghold in their flesh, they will obey what the flesh is screaming for. Sometimes, this is an addiction to drugs or food, or maybe even spending money erratically and thoughtlessly. However, it doesn't have to be an addiction for us to obey the flesh.

Most of our idols aren't golden calves or statues, but they might be different people, other places, or just about anything we give preference to or place above God. It may be as simple as any occasion that we do not choose God's desire over our fleshly desires. If it is repeated enough or when something is done in spite of God's will or His voice to us on a matter, harmful or not, that is when obeying the flesh becomes worship of something other than God.

Strongholds and addictions give voice to our fleshly desires, wounds, and pain, preferring that voice over our obedience to God or His will. I have walked this road of addiction to things other than God, and I can testify of the freedom from it through standing on God's word and prayer. *What we obey, we honor; what we honor highly, we worship.*

Of course, not all honor or obedience is a form of worship. I obey traffic laws, but I don't worship them. I honor my parents, but I don't worship them. There is a fine line at times, keeping obedience and worship in the proper perspective. As we consider this topic today, let's make sure we are mindful always to give God the first and highest place of obedience and honor and every other form of honor, obedience, preference, and priority to line up after Him.

PRAYER

Father, show me if I have anything in my life that I have placed above You. Show me in Your Word the way of freedom from those things. Help me surrender to You above those things from now on. I love You, and only You, but if something unsuspecting has crept in ahead of You or has come before You in my life, I ask for forgiveness for that. I ask for direction in correcting my acts of worship. I pray that I keep my worship to You pure and true, in spirit and truth, all my days. I pray this in the name of Jesus. Amen.

DAY 26

— OUR FRUIT OF PRAYER —

WHAT IS PRAYER?

A fuller understanding of what something *is* often comes by first understanding all the things it *is not*. So, let's look at what the Bible says prayer is not. An excellent place to start is in Romans 8:26–27:

> Likewise the Spirit also helps in our weaknesses. For we do not know what we should pray for as we ought, but the Spirit Himself makes intercession for us with groanings which cannot be uttered. Now He who searches the hearts knows what the mind of the Spirit is, because He makes intercession for the saints according to the will of God.

This scripture is essential for understanding prayer and reveals at least three layers that prayer must contain. The first layer addresses what we should pray for or pray about. The second layer is the Holy Spirit's participation in our prayers. The final layer deals with the necessity of praying for what is known to be the will of God—which is only possible by the Word of God and the Holy Spirit.

Each of these are areas a believer must come to understand and practice in their journey to our relationship with Christ. Psalm 55:17 sets a pattern for us by saying, "Evening and morning and at noon I will pray, and cry aloud, and He shall hear my voice." And 1 Thessalonians 5:17 says, "Pray without ceasing."

Obviously, we can't possibly spend every second praying in our prayer closet. Why? Because we have responsibilities in the natural. I mean, if parents did only this, literally, our kids would starve, and so would we. We are to understand that "without ceasing" means daily, moment by moment, and don't stop. Prayer is a prominent aspect of a believer's everyday life, as much a part of our lives as eating food or taking a shower. Don't stop praying.

Matthew 6:7–9 gives more insight as to what prayer should not be, saying, "When you pray, do not heap up empty phrases as the Gentiles do, for they think that they will be heard for their many words. Do not be like them, for your Father knows what you need before you ask him." The Scripture refers to the way those who were non-believers in Christ would use repeated, empty words to call out to whatever pagan god that they worshiped. It's ineffective ultimately because God is real, not fictional, fake, or mythical. We communicate with the One true living God much like we would our spouse or mother or father on earth, with complete thought, passion for, love, and genuine conversation.

As we gain an understanding of how our reconciliation in Christ established a righteous, personal relationship with God, we can then appreciate our access—now, we can talk to Him anytime! Some days, we might speak with Him for a longer time, especially when there are ongoing issues or when we need extra wisdom for decisions. It's important to know that even when we have already asked for help or understanding, returning to God again is okay! As we grow in the relationship, we come to understand that the needs we have made known to Him are not forgotten. The Bible says that we go and grow from faith to faith:

> For in it the righteousness of God is revealed from faith to faith; as it is written, "The just shall live by faith." (Romans 1:17)

There are always things we think we need or even things we think we desire. Not everything we ask for in prayer is God's will or desire for our lives. Our heart's intentions and objectives can be cloudy in some situations, and we think we want something specific. However, if we were to get that one thing, it could ruin our lives or bump us off the path of His plan for our lives. Some have set out to get these things in their flesh and later wished they had just trusted God.

When you come again in prayer, remember that God has a perfect memory. He doesn't need us to repeat it entirely but welcomes us to draw near for comfort, reassurance, and to thank Him for His answer.

When we feel pressure from situations or people to repeat the petition continuously, this can hinder our faith. Instead, drawing near and thanking God for the answer, staying in communication, and standing in faith will help us have confidence in our hearts' prayer and know that He will answer us. When we feel compelled to ask over and over and over for the same thing in prayer, that is a sure sign that we are probably not in faith to receive it, or we are not sure it is His will for us to have what we asked. God responds to our *faith.*

> What is the conclusion then? I will pray with the spirit, and I will also pray with the understanding. I will sing with the spirit, and I will also sing with the understanding. (1 Corinthians 14:15)

Obviously, we can't include a complete list of what prayer is in just one day's devotional. But we can give a good place to begin developing an excellent, practical prayer life. For example, by praying with the Holy Spirit, we can come into agreement with God on those things that are His will. God's Word is God's will. When we know God's will, we can pray in faith with confident expectation. His one answer, as a result of His will for our lives, is much better than receiving 100 things we thought we wanted when we prayed.

When we have rightly applied Scripture, in context, of course, to present the need to Him during prayer, we can rest securely in the confidence that we are praying in agreement with the will of God. Praying in the Holy Ghost is an excellent way to have that same confidence when we don't know exactly what we should be praying for in a given situation. The Bible calls the Holy Spirit our *helper*, so it is one of the functions of the Holy Spirit to help us as we pray.

Prayer is conversation and communion with God. So, we see that prayer should be continuous and conscious. Prayer is sometimes just sitting with God, telling Him how grateful you are to be able to converse and express love to Him. But prayer is also a time to get honest with ourselves before God. As we honestly open the wounds before Him, allowing examination and offering confession from a repentant heart, He can bring true transformation and healing.

God knows every detail of our situations as well as all the "whys" that are involved in them. We can't keep our true motives hidden from Him. At times when I am in prayer, He has lovingly placed His thumb of correction on an area of my life, particularly my motivation. I can only then surrender to His correction. In those times, He has even shown me motives that were hidden from my own heart's true intent. How is that possible? Because, at times, the motive of our mind can override the intent of our heart. As we trust God, He will bring understanding and correction. As we grow and mature in our faith, He requires us first to judge ourselves. Our willingness to do so according to the Word shows that we are maturing in our prayer life.

PRAYER

Father, I ask today that You keep me learning about this beautiful fruit as I gain nutrition for my spirit from our times of prayer. May I be ever learning and receiving the knowledge of Your Truth, always trusting You for understanding through Your Holy Word. Amen.

DAY 27

— OUR FRUIT OF PRAYER —

THE STRUCTURE OF PRAYER

On Day 26, we talked about what prayer is. Today, I want to discuss the structure or makeup of prayer. Some people may automatically refer to the famous scripture known as the Lord's prayer in Matthew 6:9–13, but I would like to present a fresh look.

In my understanding and study of scripture, I have found that the prayer found in Matthew Chapter 6 is a *fulfilled prayer* once Jesus completes His work on the cross and sends the Holy Ghost to us.

It's certainly a good start if you're learning to pray, and I did this, but not for long. There is an excellent pattern there, but there is no real power we can access by using just a pattern. There are many reasons that Jesus taught them this pre-Holy Spirit prayer when He did, but I won't get into those in this

121

short writing. It is a great study to take up in your additional study times.

I will say that I do start my prayers every time with honor and praise about who God is to me, but I quickly move to more effective prayer, such as those written in Ephesians 1:16–23 and Ephesians 3:14–21. These are excellent prayers for the post-resurrection church.

> [I] do not cease to give thanks for you, making mention of you in my prayers: that the God of our Lord Jesus Christ, the Father of glory, may give to you the spirit of wisdom and revelation in the knowledge of Him, the eyes of your understanding being enlightened; that you may know what is the hope of His calling, what are the riches of the glory of His inheritance in the saints, and what is the exceeding greatness of His power toward us who believe, according to the working of His mighty power which He worked in Christ when He raised Him from the dead and seated Him at His right hand in the heavenly places, far above all principality and power and might and dominion, and every name that is named, not only in this age but also in that which is to come.

> And He put all things under His feet, and gave Him to be head over all things to the

church, which is His body, the fullness of Him who fills all in all. (Ephesians 1:16–23)

For this reason I bow my knees to the Father of our Lord Jesus Christ, from whom the whole family in heaven and earth is named, that He would grant you, according to the riches of His glory, to be strengthened with might through His Spirit in the inner man, that Christ may dwell in your hearts through faith; that you, being rooted and grounded in love, may be able to comprehend with all the saints what is the width and length and depth and height— to know the love of Christ which passes knowledge; that you may be filled with all the fullness of God.

Now to Him who is able to do exceedingly abundantly above all that we ask or think, according to the power that works in us, to Him be glory in the church by Christ Jesus to all generations, forever and ever. Amen. (Ephesians 3:14–21)

I start my prayers in the morning by praying these verses and adding my pronouns to make them personal, such as using "I" or "me" in appropriate places in the verse. I pray God's

Word back to God in full faith, followed by whatever else is on my heart that morning.

Throughout the day, I will continue adding to this prayer, not starting all over, but when a situation comes to mind. For example, if I'm driving or cooking at that moment, I will begin to speak my thoughts to God. I pray out loud when possible; if I am in a place where I can't step away to talk out loud, I will pray silently in my heart. I am so glad God is the only one who can examine our thoughts and the questions in our hearts. He knows the meditations of my heart and yours.

After that, I will stay quiet and listen, and all day, I purposefully keep an open ear to listen for times when He speaks back to me. Keeping the communication open and dialogue two-way all day is essential to me. We can hear His voice in our hearts and souls, and some hear His voice audibly, although that doesn't seem to be generally as common as hearing His voice in our hearts.

God speaks to us every day, and responding to His voice when He speaks is vital to authentic communication with Him. Think about it. Doesn't it bother you a bit to be ignored when you are talking to someone? Now, maybe they don't know we are speaking to them, but if we are in an open, continuous conversation and yet being ignored, well, that is a pet peeve of mine. It is rude and inconsiderate of the relationship. How much more so with the Lord! If I don't like to be treated that way in personal relationships, I certainly wouldn't want to do that same thing to God!

Foundations

The foremost aspect and power of prayer is using the name of Jesus. Powerless prayers are ineffective. That is why I believe the Matthew Chapter 6 prayer isn't relevant today, after the resurrection of Christ. Ephesians 5:18–21 clearly tells us what God's will is for us using the name of Jesus:

> And do not be drunk with wine, in which is dissipation; but be filled with the Spirit, speaking to one another in psalms and hymns and spiritual songs, singing and making melody in your heart to the Lord, giving thanks always for all things to God the Father in the name of our Lord Jesus Christ, submitting to one another in the fear of God.

This instruction in Ephesians is crucial to believers in Christ, but it is also my foundation for using the name of Jesus in prayer. There are examples of how the disciples carried out this structure of prayer in Acts 3:6, Acts 19:5, Acts 4:18, Colossians 3:17, Mark 9:38–39, John 16:25–26, and John 20:30–31.

Sometimes, stepping away from a public space or situation is required to be effective in prayer. Many times in the Bible, Jesus employs this stepping away to pray. It was His custom to go away, to withdraw from the crowds, to be alone to speak with His Father. One place is found in Luke 11:1, "now it came to pass, as He was praying in a certain place when He ceased, that one of His disciples said to Him, "Lord, teach us to pray, as John also taught his disciples."

However, this is not the only way we are to pray. In Acts 1:14 and Acts 2:42, the Bible describes another place we are to pray: the place of agreement! Acts 1:14 says, "These all continued with one accord in prayer and supplication, with the women and Mary the mother of Jesus, and with His brothers." In Acts 2:42, it says, "And they continued steadfastly in the apostles' doctrine and fellowship, in the breaking of bread, and in prayers." Notice that in both situations of prayer, they were in *one accord* or agreement, also called unity. In unity with other believers is a Biblical structure for prayer.

The last important structure must be the motive of our heart. For example, forgiveness of others is a requirement to receive forgiveness from God for yourself. Forgiveness is a fundamental pillar of the Christian walk of living as a son or daughter of God. The same is true about love and prayer. The prayer of faith works only by Love. Matthew 5:44–45 says, "But I say to you, love your enemies, bless those who curse you, do good to those who hate you, and pray for those who spitefully use you and persecute you, that you may be sons of your Father in heaven; for He makes His sun rise on the evil and on the good, and sends rain on the just and on the unjust."

In the same way that natural children mirror and mimic their parents, we should be the same way with our heavenly Father, reflecting His actions and will. These are keys to answered prayer. The Bible calls this *abiding in Christ.* John 15:7 (emphasis added) says, "If you abide in Me, and My words abide in you, you will ask what you desire, and [because you abide] it shall be done for you."

This lesson is not all-encompassing but is an excellent start to developing our fruit of prayer. Let's recap this longer-than-normal study on specific structures for prayer:

- Start by praying one or both of the specific prayers from Ephesians 1:16–23 and Ephesians 3:14–21.

- Pray other passages of Scripture according to the need or situation.

- Continue the prayer or conversation with God throughout the day.

- Make time in prayer to listen to His voice.

- Use the power given to us in prayer by praying in the name of Jesus.

- Step away in order to be alone and pray in certain situations.

- Pray in unity with fellow believers and in agreement with God's Word.

- Pray from the posture of love (not arrogance or manipulation of the situation).

- Forgive others as the Father God has forgiven you in Christ.

- Abide in Christ by adopting His character and actions toward those around you.

If this basic structure is used when you pray, your prayers will be powerful and effective.

PRAYER

Father, may my prayer times be holy communication with You. Prompt me to remain primarily quiet and to listen, and never stumble through the act by begging. May our prayer engagements refresh both You and me, encourage both You and me, and leave space for us both to speak clearly and freely to each other. I ask this in the name of Jesus Christ. Amen.

DAY 28

— OUR FRUIT OF PRAYER —

OUR PRAYER OF CONFESSION

Is any among you suffering? Let him pray. Is anyone cheerful? Let him sing palms. Is anyone among you sick? Let him call for the elders of the church, and let them pray over him, anointing him with oil in the name of the Lord. And the prayer of faith will heal him. (James 5:13–16)

Our confession consists of the words that we speak. Our confession and conversation provide a good indicator of what we fear or struggle with. It's humbling to our natural pride to expose any weakness in our character, but the reality is that God already knows all about those weaknesses. Paying attention to our words exposes those fears and hangups *to us*.

Watch and pray, that ye enter not into temptation: the spirit indeed is willing, but the flesh is weak. (Matthew 26:41 KJV)

Watch ye and pray, lest ye enter into temptation. The spirit truly is ready, but the flesh is weak. (Mark 14:38 KJV)

First, we have not arrived and are not yet all-knowing and all-understanding, perfect and wise. That is waiting for us in heaven, but here on earth, we will clearly struggle. Other people can see some of our struggles. But most of our fears and struggles can only be seen by God, who reveals the heart of the battle to us so that we can be free from them.

Confession is also speaking up or out about our own faults and sins. Exposing sin isn't framing yourself as an immoral or sinful Christian. It's revealing your clear understanding that you are a human, experiencing complex, even embarrassing human issues. But knowing I am human and admitting I am human in failures are sometimes two very different things. Exposing our own sin is humbling.

So, in either use, our confession is a blessing. The pressure and relief that comes with confession of sin is freeing. Jesus came to set us completely free, which includes freedom from hiding things. Hiding an issue and not exposing it leads a person further down a deadly path of destruction and further away from healing and growth in God. I learned this the hard way, so I hope to save you the same hardship by sharing honestly here. True humility is this ability to admit you were wrong in an area and are actively seeking to make it right.

PRAYER

Father, give us the desire to be people who can be trusted with another's confession of sin and fears. Keep our hearts pure, saturated with love, and without judgment of others. Remind us also to confess our faults one to another—to trusted believers—repenting of the things we need to be free and separated from. I pray this in the name of Jesus. Amen.

DAY 29

— OUR FRUIT OF PRAYER —

OUR PRAYER OF THANKFULNESS

Being thankful and expressing gratitude are key aspects of prayer. Thankfulness is mentioned several times in the Bible in connection with prayer. Here are a few passages to look at:

> Continue earnestly in prayer, being vigilant in it with thanksgiving. (Colossians 4:2)

> Rejoice always, pray without ceasing, in everything give thanks; for this is the will of God in Christ Jesus for you. (1 Thessalonians 5:16–18)

After I pray the Scripture out loud and tell God how great and awesome He is, I move into a time of speaking of all the most recent things and people I am thankful for. I spend time thanking Him for the previous things I have requested and am still expecting to come to pass.

One testimony of the power of prayer and standing in expectation with thanksgiving is from a time when I required healing in my body. I had developed a large tumor on my face, which had continued to grow over several years. I had undergone CT scans and ultrasounds, which monitored and measured it from year to year. By the fourth year, it had become quite noticeable, especially looking at me straight on. In fact, it had almost doubled in size from the first CT scan to that fourth year.

I had been weighing the option of surgery to remove the tumor, but the surgery would have been a long 3-hour process. In the doctor's opinion, there was a high possibility of nerve damage in my face as a result of the procedure; still, the doctor felt the surgery was my only real option.

One day during that fourth year, I remember being busy with many things. During these activities, I happened to reach up and touch my face in the area where the tumor had been growing. I suddenly discovered that the Lord had wholly and miraculously removed that tumor! I just knew it was a miracle.

Yes, I had plenty of questions during those four years of standing in faith as time progressed and the tumor grew. But continually and in complete gratitude, I thanked the Lord for His healing answer and miracle. Still today, I am never ashamed to be loud as I praise Him, thanking Him for removing it—with no surgery and no medication, just simple faith with thanksgiving and honest prayers.

Other things in my life come to my mind now that have been just as marvelous, many beautiful things that God has done and shown me. I imagine there are things now that might also come to mind for you if you allow them to. These are the moments when we should stop whatever we are doing at that moment, no matter where we are, and thank God! The truth is, through it all, God has been so good because it is His nature. He is a good God.

A miracle is humbling. But every answer to prayer is worthy of thanks! He is faithful. His mercy endures forever! There is always something you can be thankful for, so start small if you must. Just be grateful every day—thanksgiving is the victory in our prayer life!

PRAYER

Father, help us to understand and see the greatness of your nature. Show us how You are the good, good Father God. Show us ways we can demonstrate Your goodness to those around us. Remind us as we go about our day of the beautiful things You have done in our lives. Remind us of the miracles, provisions of every kind, and relationships that have been restored, Father. We can always praise You, at any time, anywhere, for all the myriad of ways You help us—You rescue and recover us from more than we know! Keep our hearts in a thankful position with praise at the front of our minds, Lord! I ask this in the name of Jesus. Amen.

Day 30

— OUR FRUIT OF PRAYER —

Prayer of Solidarity and Peace

Praying in unity and as the body of Christ results in God's blessing and peaceful lifestyles. Peace through effective prayer is the theme of the Scriptures below:

> Be careful for nothing, but in everything by prayer and supplication with thanksgiving let your requests be made known unto God. And the peace of God which passeth all understanding, shall keep your hearts and minds through Christ Jesus. (Philippians 4:6–7 KJV)

> Continue in prayer, and watch in the same with thanksgiving, withal praying also for us, that God would open unto us a door of utter-

ance to speak the mystery of Christ, for which I
am also in bonds. (Colossians 4:2–3 KJV)

God calls His children to be of one mind and one accord.

> Be of the same mind toward one another. Do
> not set your mind on high things, but associate
> with the humble. Do not be wise in your own
> opinion. (Romans 12:16)

As this happens, influential and significant results are seen
as vibrant, strong churches grow and families flourish. Gov-
ernments begin working smoothly for the benefit of their people because positions are filled with Christ-minded people.
Progress and prosperity come to education, the media, and the
marketplace because the Righteous reign, which significantly
impacts the culture around us.

True unity and abiding peace are precious, and we see in
the Scriptures how there is one guaranteed way to possess it.

> I exhort therefore, that, first of all, suppli-
> cations, prayers, intercessions, and giving of
> thanks be made for all men; for kings and all
> that are in authority; that we may lead a quiet
> and peaceable life in all godliness and honesty.
> (1 Timothy 2:1–2 KJV)

PRAYER

Father, thank you for the reward of peace for our unity. Help us as a whole Body of Christ to understand Your heart for unity. Teach us how to keep peace and solidarity throughout our country, cities, and homes. I ask this in Jesus' name. Amen.

DAY 31

— OUR FRUIT OF PRAYER —
GOD'S RESPONSE TO OUR PRAYER

God is responsive to the prayers of His people. He loves to communicate and fellowship with each one of His children. We learn of Him and His love through these times we spend with Him alone. Don't ever feel that He doesn't hear our prayers; the Bible says God hears the prayers of His own:

> The Lord hath heard my supplication; the Lord will receive my prayer. (Psalm 6:9 KJV)

> If my people, which are called by my name, shall humble themselves, and pray and seek my face, and turn from their wicked ways; then will I hear from heaven, and will forgive their

sin, and will heal their land. (2 Chronicles 7:14 KJV)

For the eyes of the Lord are on the righteous, and His ears are open to their prayers; but the face of the Lord is against those who do evil. (1 Peter 3:12)

The Lord is far from the wicked; but heareth the prayer of the righteous. (Proverbs 15:29 KJV)

God will not turn away from us if we bring Him difficult prayers or confessions of shameful things we have done. He desires that we freely come to Him, seeking Him and finding forgiveness. He is full of mercy and compassion toward us.

If I regard iniquity [only] in my heart, the Lord will not hear me: But verily God hath heard me; he hath attended to the voice of my prayer. Blessed be God, which hath not turned away my prayer, nor his mercy from me. (Psalm 66:18–20 KJV; emphasis added)

One of the infinitely awesome things about God is that He is always available to us! He doesn't sleep, and He is never beyond reach or where He can't hear our cries for help or our shouts of praise in victory. When we purpose to get quiet before Him and wait for Him, we will hear what He wants to say to us.

Making prayer a two-way conversation with God helps expose some very revealing things about our hearts and lives within His source of comfort. This communion in prayer is a fount of wisdom in times when we feel stuck and the best advice. God doesn't just hear our prayers; He sees our hearts when we pray. He already knows the things we can't seem to say for whatever reason to Him or ourselves.

I encourage you to be brave anyway and say those things to Him. He knows all the reasons we ask for what we ask for in prayer, and He doesn't hold back. He answers us as we pause, make space for Him, and wait for Him to minister healing to our hearts.

A final encouragement is that it is wise to respond quickly back to God, especially when He asks us to do something or when He responds to our prayers for guidance by directing our choices. Often, we might think we are waiting on His answer when, in reality, He is waiting for us to respond to His directive and guidance through the Holy Spirit.

Many times, our hearts or minds are too crowded with thoughts or fears, so we miss what He says the first time. If this seems to be the case with your communion in prayer, get quiet. Find a quiet place and ask Him again for His response. He loves us. He isn't going to be angry because we missed it. Faith pleases God. He is pleased with our faith that when we ask, He answers.

PRAYER

Father, thank you for being approachable and full of mercy when we come to you in our times of need or seeking forgiveness. I pray that we mimic Your gracious responses when we need to relate to others in their time of need. I pray we learn to respond quickly and obediently to Your voice and commands for our lives. Thank you for always being there and not turning away from us. Thank you for not being distant from us at any given time. I love You, and I love it when You help me make my life decisions. I am so thankful to learn that things always turn out better when I turn to You. Amen.

NOTES

1   "Stand." Merriam-Webster.com Dictionary. Accessed November 13, 2024, https://www.merriam-webster.com/dictionary/stand.

2   "Stand." Merriam-Webster.com Thesaurus. Accessed November 18, 2024, https://www.merriam-webster.com/thesaurus/stand.

3   "Stand." Dictionary.com. Accessed November 18, 2024. https://www.dictionary.com/browse/stand.

4   "Resist." WordReference.com Dictionary of English, accessed August 21, 2024, https://www.wordreference.com/definition/resist.

5   "Resist." Oxford English Dictionary, accessed August 21, 2024, https://www.oed.com/dictionary/resist

6   Tedrow-Wynn, Mary Ellen. "Psalm 30:5 (Psalm Treasure #54)." And Like Gold Refined Again, May 23, 2024. https://likegoldrefined-again.wordpress.com/2024/05/23/psalm-305-psalm-treasure-54/.

7   "H7445 - rnānâ - Strong's Hebrew Lexicon (kjv)." Blue Letter Bible. Accessed 7 Sep, 2024. https://www.blueletterbible.org/lexicon/h7445/kjv/wlc/0-1/

8   "H7442 - rānan - Strong's Hebrew Lexicon (kjv)." Blue Letter Bible. Accessed 7 Sep, 2024. https://www.blueletterbible.org/lexicon/h7442/kjv/wlc/0-1/

9   "heritage." *Webster's New World College Dictionary*, 5th ed., 2016, p. 680.

10   "heritage," Oxford Advanced Learner's Dictionary, accessed November 14, 2024, https://www.oxfordlearnersdictionaries.com/definition/english/heritage.

MEET THE AUTHOR

Author Tamra Ingram-Curry was born in the beautiful Ozark Mountains, where she continues to reside with her husband and family. Before making a U-turn in life into writing and editing, Tamra was a hairdresser for 20 years.

The new direction followed her obtaining a Bachelor of Arts in ministry and furthering that education with a Bachelor of Science in Professional and Technical Writing and a Bachelor of Science in Psychology from Missouri State University.

In addition to writing and editing, Tamra expresses her creativity in painting and photography as a fabric artist. However, her passion is found in playing drums, and she is featured on a music album by the band Laus Perennis entitled *That Place*, which can be found on iTunes® or Spotify®.

As a writer of creative nonfiction, poetry, and the use of photography, her writings teach and encourage positive lifestyle habits after trauma response and recovery.

One of her works of poetry, *The Wonder of His Hands*, is featured in the 2016 compilation by Eber and Wein Publishing titled *Beyond the Sea: Mystique*. Additional works by Tamra Ingram-Curry include her published book, *Renew*, featuring a bit of her photography, along with works of poetry. *Renew*, along with this devotional and companion journal series, *Our Fruits of Christianity*, is currently available on Amazon. For additional copies or to contact the author directly:

Tamra Ingram-Curry

P.O. Box 415

Valley Springs, AR 72682